"Ready to upgrade your financial game? LADYSHARK shows you how to break free from outdated money myths and swim towards a brighter financial future."

Ted Gonder, Cofounding CEO of Moneythink, Forbes 30Under30 in Finance

"Tired of playing by someone else's rules? Chrissy will help you unleash your inner Ladyshark so you can become a real estate boss and run your own life."

Susie Hollands, Founder & CEO of Vingt Paris, a leading European real estate firm

"Chrissy is the real deal: A self-made millionaire who operates with business savvy from a place of heart. Opening doors wide for people without gold star educations or networks, and offering them a path to success, financial freedom, and personal fulfillment."

MeiMei Fox, 2x NYTimes bestselling author & FORBES Contributor

TSPA

Chrissy Grigoropoulos
Ladyshark: *How to become a millionaire in your 30s*

GLG Publishing
Copyright © 2024 by Chrissy Grigoropoulos
First Edition

Hardcover ISBN 979-8-9901593-0-3
Softcover ISBN 979-8-9901593-1-0
eBook ISBN 979-8-9901593-2-7

Printed in Canada

Book Design | Petya Tsankova
Editors | Jen Tate and MeiMei Fox
Author Portrait Photography | Darren Harman @harmancreatives
Publishing Support | TSPA The Self Publishing Agency, Inc.

LADY SHARK

HOW TO BECOME A MILLIONAIRE IN YOUR 30s

Chrissy Grigoropoulos, Esq.

To my parents, who taught me that anything is possible,
and encouraged me to become a Ladyshark.

And to my husband and children,
who are the reason I will always be one!

Table of Contents

INTRODUCTION:

What It Takes to Be A Ladyshark

If you're reading this, then the part about making millions in your 30s must have caught your attention, right?

That's great, because I'm all about making money! The money is the motive. We're talking stability and financial freedom. And we'll definitely get to that part, because I'm a true believer in being able to support yourself to live the lifestyle you desire.

But I'm about much more than that. And I bet you are, too.

So, let's start with the obvious question: What exactly is a Ladyshark? We've got to agree on that before we do anything else!

A Ladyshark is someone who has a burning desire to succeed. A Ladyshark does things her own way, not the way society tells her to. She's not afraid to put herself out there…her authentic self.

A Ladyshark leaves people in awe of her drive, her indomitable will, and her achievements. But she also strives for a mindset that includes others, wins allies, and makes a positive impact on the world.

And just to be clear: Being a Ladyshark isn't about gender. Anyone can be a Ladyshark. Because being a Ladyshark is all about your spirit. Your vibe. It's about audacity. It's about courage. It's about relentlessly pursuing your dreams. It's about staying hungry and making success a lifelong journey instead of a destination.

How do I know all of this? Because I'm a Ladyshark. I have what it takes. And I bet you do, too.

Who Am I?

You may have seen me on the back of buses advertising my law firm. Or on TV talking about making money without earning a college degree that leaves you buried under mounds of debt. Or even commenting on the latest news from the perspective of a lawyer.

If you live in the New York Tri-State Area, you may have seen "Chrissy Grigoropoulos, Esq." on billboards advertising my services as a personal injury and worker's compensation attorney.

If you live on the internet, you may have watched my YouTube videos or followed my Instagram page.

And if you don't have a clue who I am but you're intrigued by the idea of becoming a success story, keep reading!

I'm a completely self-made woman.

To break down some of my credibility, I graduated from high school at age 16 and college at 19. I got myself into and through law school when no one thought I would or could. And I gradu-ated by the age of 25. In fact, some people joke that I'm the real life Elle Woods from *Legally Blonde* (you know, the classic movie starring Reese Witherspoon as an attorney all dolled up in pink?). I'll take it! She's an OG Ladyshark, known by many, for sure.

And because I'm a Ladshark, I didn't stop there. I also started several booming businesses – a law firm, The Grigoropoulos Law Group PLLC, a real estate company, Property Shark Realty, Inc, an Independent Medical Exam defending agency, IME Sharks, Inc, and others. Currently, these businesses are earning me millions.

And because I'm a Ladyshark, I didn't stop there, either. I man-ifested the single most important thing to me – a family. I'm a proud wife to a sexy and successful man, the mother of two young children (so far), and a devoted daughter to my loving parents.

Because I'm a Ladyshark, I believe you can have it all: Career triumph and personal life fulfillment.

Because I'm a Ladyshark, I know *you* can achieve all of this with-out cheating the system and while still being a kind and generous person.

Not only that, but you can do it without a degree from a fancy college, a trust fund, or "the right network" from birth. You can even do it if, at this very moment, you're feeling down on your luck, hopeless, buried in debt, and ready to give up.

Anyone who wants to become a Ladyshark can. Anyone!

It means freeing your own fierce and fearless spirit. Opening your eyes to the opportunities all around you. And committing to a life of success and thinking outside the box…which you're already doing just by reading this book!

You can binge-read *Ladyshark* on a lazy Sunday afternoon, on your next vacation, on the train home from work, or on a plane on your way to kick some business ass. Or you can keep it in your bag to read between classes, on your bedside table for a jolt of inspiration each morning, or on your phone for those precious moments when your kids are napping.

This book is the perfect gift for anyone who wants to help other people in their lives become Ladysharks – GED or high school grad, college student or graduate, people looking to make a career change, people struggling with debt, or maybe colleagues and best friends who are hungry for inspiration.

Becoming a Ladyshark isn't rocket science. Truly anyone can do it. But it takes hard work. Serious dedication. And a deep belief in how amazing you are, and what you have the capacity to do. The sky's the limit!

I'll kick things off by telling you more of my own story about how I became a Ladyshark. Then it's your turn to start your journey to success!

I've put together eight steps you can take to help you tap into the Ladyshark that already exists within you. You can mix and match these chapters, read them backwards, or circle back to them whenever you need a pick-me-up.

At the end, you'll find a Ladyshark Journey Workbook to help you ask yourself some critical questions. You can use the process of answering them to transform your thoughts into a plan of action.

I've thrown in some extra goodies for you, too. Scattered throughout the book you'll learn about Ladysharks you should know, some traits Ladysharks share with real sharks, and most importantly, some fantastic Greek sayings and life lessons I've picked up from my father, a self-made Ladyshark if ever there was one. His advice to me over the years adds some actual "big fat Greek" life experience to the mix!

My father is an extraordinary human – one of the people I admire most in the world. He immigrated to America without speaking a word of English and not even $20 in his pocket. And he Ladysharked his way into construction and then real estate development. Despite his 5th grade education, in contrast to my doctorate, he is, and always will be, smarter than me. How could I not share the wealth of knowledge that he so generously has shared with me throughout my life?!

His words of wisdom have helped me again and again, so I'm betting they'll be useful for you, too. Stick them on your fridge, make them your daily mantras – whatever works for you.

Plus, I'll talk about some of my favorite big time Ladysharks out there. The ones who've been there, done that. Shattered ceilings and defied odds. They'll fire you up and show you what's possible, because although cliche, even the impossible is possible for Ladysharks!

Being a Ladyshark means rewriting the rules. It means defining success on your own terms.

It's not just a title; it's a mindset. So let's reset your mind, reboot your life together, and make your wildest dreams a reality!

HOW I BECAME
A LADYSHARK

I decided that I was going to be a lawyer when I was seven years old. Now you may ask, and rightly so, "How the hell did you know what a lawyer *was* when you were seven?"

I'll tell you.

My father was born in Greece. At 17 years old, with only a 5th grade education, he jumped on a boat and left the only life he knew, bidding farewell to his parents and three older siblings to seek out success instead of going into the army. He came to America speaking only Greek, and built himself up from nothing. By the time I was 7, my father was running his own construction company, as well as buying and fixing up houses and buildings to rent or sell.

One awful day when I was young, one of my father's tenants left the gas on and there was an explosion. The entire home blew up.

That afternoon, my mom got a call from the fire department telling her that my father had been severely burned. It turned out that it was one of his employees who'd been burned, not my father. But you can imagine the intensity of the situation in my house. My mother was screaming, and I could feel the panic in the air.

Naturally, that event was the beginning of a huge lawsuit. We're talking litigation, insurance claims, arson accusations, all of that. It was a terrible time and a complicated experience for my father, especially since his English was limited. Keeping track of all of the legal documents and communication was a nightmare.

A few weeks later, when he was asked to appear for a deposition, I went with him. Even though I was young, sometimes he brought me along to help translate what I could, and he was always my best friend. I remember this day so clearly. I had a conversation in Greek with him while we rode in an elevator.

Dad: This lawyer cost us so much money. He told me $500 or something an hour. You should be a lawyer one day.

7-year-old Me: Really? What do lawyers do?

Dad: They fight.

7-year-old Me: They fight?

Dad: They fight all day. And they make a lot of money.

7-year-old Me: I like to fight! I like money! I'm going to be a lawyer when I grow up.

(Note: My father debates me about this story now, insisting that the whole lawyer idea was mine from the get go. But this is my book, so my version wins!)

Flash forward to me as an adolescent. I'd grown up in Queens, going to public school until I was about 15. Then we moved to the middle-of-nowhere Long Island, where I dealt with some serious culture shock coming from the urban lifestyle I was used to. There were no friends I knew from kindergarten, nor anyone who knew me, the real me.

That's when becoming a lawyer really became a driving force for me. By that point, my father was saying things like:

You should always be independent.
Study hard, work hard, and you will be a lawyer.
You'll be able to make your own money.
You won't need anyone to support you.

It was around this time that I decided it was less important for me to have a big group of friends than it was to be done with my education quickly. With college and law school still ahead of me, I didn't want to waste any time.

I went straight to my high school guidance counselor to figure out a plan for how to finish high school fast. It turned out this would mean skipping lunch, picking up an extra class to pack my schedule, and letting go of the free periods and fun everyone around me seemed to be having. But getting strategic like this was how I graduated from high school early, when I was only 16.

Then I tore through college just as quickly, graduating when I was 19 by taking classes during the summer and over winter breaks. I knew law school was going to be really hard, so I just put my head down and plowed through my pre-reqs as fast as I possibly could.

Wow, was I right. Law school was brutal. One of the hardest things I've ever had to do. I'll get into more of that later in the book. For now, let's just say there were several times when I wasn't sure how I was going to make it to graduation.

But I did! Then I spent some time working for law firms to actually learn the ins and outs of the profession. First was criminal defense. Next was insurance and municipality defense. And finally, plaintiff personal injury chose me. That's how I became a personal injury and workers compensation attorney.

What exactly is a personal injury and workers' compensation attorney? I'm glad you asked. (I'm a lawyer. Of course I love answering questions!)

I like to think of myself as an educator. An advocate for people going through a terrible time in life after an accident. I help them through the process of seeking medical treatment and fighting for their right to compensation for their pain and suffering. It's a little bit like parenting someone through a legal case – letting them know every step of the way what's going on, what to expect, and what their options are.

And honestly, it also demands a lot of tedious work that you cannot drop the ball on. What most people don't realize about personal injury law is that we work for free until we reach a settlement for you. Yes. You heard me correctly, a personal injury lawyer doesn't get paid anything until their client does. This can mean years of investing unpaid legal work before seeing any money.

Eventually, in 2016 at age 28, I started my own personal injury and workers' compensation law firm. And by law firm I mean that at first, it was just one paralegal and me in a little office inside of another small company. Today, we have three of our own offices, five attorneys and counting, and an additional staff of 15.

Here's what I will tell you about being a Ladyshark and starting your own company. You can't sit still. You can't wait for people to come knocking on your door, because they're never coming. You can't stay home on your sofa. You can't sleep in. You can't party too much. You have to keep thinking outside the box, because if you don't, you'll just end up doing what everyone else is doing. You won't stand out.

Most importantly, you must keep your word and deliver everything you say you will. You have to be relentless. You have to keep trying and trying and trying. It's never enough.

Right now, I'm taking online classes on how to be a better business owner. I'm good at being a lawyer, but even after almost eight years of running my own company, I still feel new to running a business and haven't mastered it as of yet. It's a journey, remember? Not a destination.

No matter how strong you start off, if you don't deliver what you're promising, there will be no year two, no year three, and so on. You have to be someone who can actually deliver results. Who can do what they say they're going to do. You have to have an insatiable hunger to succeed. Failure is not an option!

I used to tell myself, "When I have $100,000 in the bank, that will mean I'm successful. That will mean I don't have to worry." But you know what? My payroll is nearly $300,000 a month now. As you succeed, you have to keep striving for more.

I sacrificed a lot in my youth. I never went to a high school party. I didn't do a lot of things that people around me thought of as "normal." Maybe I didn't need those things? Maybe I was just really, really focused on becoming a lawyer?

I tell you all of this not to brag about myself or my life or my journey. But to promise you that if I can do it, if I can be a Ladyshark, so can you!

My father arrived in America as an immigrant with no assets but his street smarts, his work ethic, his kindness to others, and a firm belief in the American Dream. He encouraged me as I worked my way up the ladder, without the benefit of wealthy parents or a fancy education or an impressive network, to become the successful business woman, wife and mother I am today.

I share my story to inspire you. If I can be a Ladyshark, so can you. Believe it, baby!

Now let's take a look at the eight steps I took, which anyone in any industry of any age and any gender can take in order to be a Ladyshark: A true success.

HOW YOU CAN BECOME A LADYSHARK

STEP 1:

Act Like a Ladyshark

Acting like a Ladyshark means leaning into ambition and the unwavering belief in your own potential to achieve greatness – no matter what other people think. And pushing past weak moments, knowing you're destined for success if you push hard enough!

It's all about motivating yourself by figuring out what drives you, looking for ways to fix problems, and not taking no for an answer. That way, you can seize opportunities as you navigate life's challenges on your road to success!

My father would say...

Be bold - Whatever you want, look for it. Work at it and you will find it. Remember, if it was easy everyone would do it.

For a Ladyshark that means...

If you're shy about asking for what you want, that's on you. Don't be shy. You risk stunting your own growth. Ask for what you want. Work hard. No askie, no gettie!

I went to law school in the Midwest, but I'm an East Coast girl to the core.

So, while I was heading to class in my sparkling pink, purple, orange and turquoise velour Juicy Couture suit, my Air Maxes or Jordans, my long black (at that time) hair, and my perfectly maintained French acrylic nails...most of my classmates were cruising campus dressed up like corporate attorneys, wearing crisp white button-down tops and slacks in a limited spectrum of brown, black and gray. I definitely stood out.

By 22, I'd worked hard and saved enough money to buy a car. Of course I chose a used Porsche Cayenne and had it tinted and blacked out. I was rocking the Mob Boss look way before it became trendy, and many of my classmates seemed threatened by that.

Every time I'd go home for a week to visit my family, I'd get back to school and hear that rumors were going around... People saying that I'd failed out.

I felt like an outsider most of the time. It was obvious that some of my classmates were rooting against me. Sometimes, I even heard them whisper things like, "How the hell is that girl still here? I can't believe she hasn't dropped out yet!"

That's when I started asking myself:

Who are they to judge me?
Because I don't look the way they think a lawyer should look?
Because I don't talk the way they think a lawyer should talk?
Why not me?

I was passing all the same classes they were! (Well, most of the time. But hey, nobody's perfect. And "D's get degrees," right? As long as you only get one!)

Here's what I learned from all of that: Ladysharks don't judge others. As far as I'm concerned, if you're hungry enough, if you want something bad enough, then you can have it. You can be whatever you want to be. Why not you?!

Be prepared to suffer a bit, though. The things that come easy don't usually have as much depth or longevity to them.

EMBRACE A 'WHY NOT ME?' PHILOSOPHY

No matter where you are in your personal and professional journey, now is the time to start acting like a Ladyshark. Stay hungry!

Maybe you're struggling financially or on welfare? That doesn't mean you can't be a Ladyshark. It just means you're fighting your way to the top right now.

Stop asking, Why me? And start asking, Why not me?

If you're a stripper, does that disqualify you from being a Ladyshark? Hell, no! Maybe one day you'll own your strip club like a Ladyshark!

If you've grown up in the foster care system, does that mean you'll never have a family, stability and a high-paying job? No way!

Some of the most successful entrepreneurs and motivational speakers out there are people who have come from nothing and know exactly what it takes to thrive in the face of adversity.

Anyone who claims you can't achieve what you want to achieve is just judging you, projecting their insecurities, and putting you in a box – which they have no right to do.

It *still* happens to me.

Just the other day, I walked into a deposition dressed in a standard suit – a skirt with a blazer over it. And sure, I'd added a rhinestone-embellished button-down top so I could own the look. My hair and face were nicely done, and I was even carrying a Birkin bag. I looked sharp!

But when I entered the room, one of the defendants gave me the old up-and-down a few times and said in a loud whisper, "When is the lawyer coming?" He immediately assumed the lawyer could not be me.

I walked directly over to where they were sitting and introduced myself, "Hello, I'm plaintiff's counsel."

My adversary's jaw dropped. I guess he thought I was the court reporter. I knew he was thinking, "How could this girl be a lawyer?" Right? Just like my law school classmates had always said.

All I could do was think to myself, "There they go again, underestimating me. Well, do so at your own peril!"

There's just not much we can do about other people's judgments. But we can ignore them.

Oh yes, and did I mention that we won that case? After the deposition, we settled for nearly seven figures! Take that, trolls!

Hey, it's normal to doubt yourself, especially when you're trying new things, venturing into uncharted waters, stepping into places where you might not fit the traditional mold.

A Ladyshark can transform that doubt simply by asking herself, "Why *not* me?" Recognize that your journey is valid, regardless of how you dress, where you come from, or what other people expect of you.

GET MOTIVATED

Motivation is the fuel that drives a Ladyshark.

I'm a business owner. And I have two young children who rarely sleep at night. So, yeah, sometimes I want to sit my ass at home and zone out to Netflix. Maybe a lot of the time! Sometimes I don't want to get out of bed, don't want to go to my office, and don't even want to look at another human. I get tired like everybody else.

But those are the times when, I've learned, you really do have to "fake it til you make it." Do it authentically, though. Sometimes you have to go through the motions, even when you don't want to. That's part of being an entrepreneur, being a boss, being a Ladyshark.

Because whether you work for someone else or employees work for you, there are other people relying on you. People you're responsible to or for, sometimes both.

You're going to have to do things you don't always want to do. Being successful means making sacrifices along the way. Sometimes that will mean not getting enough sleep. In fact, most of the time you may only get a fraction of the sleep that "normal people" get.

Other times, it will mean putting up with an endless string of frustrating, low-vibrational people. In the end, what matters is that you have a job to do and a ladder of success to keep climbing.

My advice is to think about what pushes you forward. What's going to get you moving when you're exhausted or facing obstacles? You have to learn how to encourage yourself.

What do I do when I'm faced with tough situations or moments of weakness? I think about my father. I ask myself, "What would Spiro do in this situation?" Then I try to channel a little something from him –- his wisdom, his fearlessness, his drive – and transform it into action, motivating myself to push forward.

So, start asking yourself, "WWALD? What would a Ladyshark do?" And use that to tap into your relentless drive.

You may not want to, but you must. Because following your vision in order to achieve your goals means relying on an unwavering commitment to yourself. You can't give up. Again, failure is not an option!

FIND YOUR FOCUS

There's no reason you can't do anything you want to do if you're focused and dedicated. Be anything you want to be – from a lawyer to a doctor to a stock broker, entrepreneur or business owner.

Sure, it's easy to get discouraged and say things like:

I wouldn't even know where to start.
I don't have any money.
I don't have good credit.
I don't have this.
I don't have that.

And to that I say…You've got to take it step by step. One foot in front of the other to start your journey.

What kind of kick-ass Ladyshark do you want to be?
Why do you want to do it?
What's the end result you're looking for?

I totally understand how hard it is to clearly identify what it is you really want. It's tough to plan out how you're going to get somewhere if you don't know why you're going there in the first place.

As I've mentioned, I found my focus when I was a little girl. I decided I wanted to be a lawyer. But that was only the first step in finding my focus. No one in my family had even graduated from college, let alone gotten a doctorate.

I grew up watching Law and Order, so I started out hungry to be a criminal lawyer, because, I thought, they put the "guilty" guys in jail. They keep the "not guilty" guys out of jail. And they looked good doing it. Perfect for me, right?

So after law school, I tried doing some defense work. But I realized pretty quickly that the salary wasn't what I was looking for. It didn't make for a sustainable lifestyle after all of my law school suffering. And there weren't many opportunities for me to grow as fast as my ambition demanded. It was time to try something else.

I ended up finding my focus through a process of elimination. I didn't want to do divorce law. I didn't want to do landlord/tenant or property law. I thought to myself, "If I can keep people out of jail, then surely I should be able to help defend people being sued for money because of an accident!" And that's how I ended up in personal injury law. I started by doing personal injury defense.

You may not know 100% what you want to do yet. And that's OK.

My advice is to find something that you enjoy, while also thinking about what you want from your lifestyle. Ask yourself:

What is my dream 5 year plan?
Where do I want to be in 10 years?

You have to be able to picture what you want out of your life in order to figure out what your next step is.

If you're living in an apartment, at home with your parents, or with a roommate out of obligation…if you're living just within your means, paycheck to paycheck, and you know you don't want your life to stay that way, then it's time to make a plan. If you want "success" – in the traditional sense of a high income, nice house, stylish car – then you have to be passionate about what you do. Passion breeds success.

BE A FIXER

I work well under pressure, in part because of my upbringing. To me, being a fixer means being good at problem solving. Both of my parents are problem solvers, so in my family, it's an inherited trait. I learned pretty quickly to be a fixer and it has served me well, in good times and bad.

My mom was in the hospital a few years ago, right when I had first started my law firm and had no free time whatsoever. The doctors did a chest X-ray and saw something alarming. They implied that it was bad news, but wouldn't give us straight answers. It was terrifying for our family – especially my mom, who had survived cancer while I was in law school by having one of her kidneys removed.

No doctor was straight with us, which was incredibly frustrating. After hours of pestering and waiting, I finally got a doctor to sit down with me for a conversation. She explained that they wanted to schedule a PET scan, a scan of the body for cancer, to make sure they fully understood what was wrong, but that was going to take weeks. My family needed answers now. This was a problem I needed to fix.

I started asking specific details about the X-ray, but she just kept saying, "Well, I can't confirm that for sure." So I had to get creative, which meant going into lawyer mode and cross examining the doctor.

I asked her, "OK, has there ever been a case where you've seen all the things on an X-ray like you've seen on my mother's and it *wasn't* cancer?"

She sighed. "No," she admitted. Heartbreakingly, my problem was solved.

After over three hours of waiting to speak to the doctor, I finally got an answer: The "C word" was once again a reality. But at least now that we had a diagnosis, we were able to go into fixer mode and start making plans immediately..

No sad ending here, thank God and all the spirits of the universe! My mom is still with us, fighting the good fight seven plus years later.

As a teenager and young adult, I was always the designated driver, the superstar friend who showed up no matter what, fixing things, getting my friends home, being the advice guru. When I started working, I became that kind of go-to person for my employers, too.

Even if I didn't know how to do something – like file a brief or take a deposition – my response was always, "Sure, throw me to the wolves, I'll figure it out." That attitude has been a huge help to me in my career, because I've been someone my bosses and colleagues can rely on, someone eager for a challenge and ready to impress.

Whenever I'm faced with a problem at work, my approach is pretty simple. In fact, I think I learned it in math class in elementary school, and I still use it all the time: Test. Check. Revise.

When I try something new, when I'm trying to fix something – first I test it.

Then I check to see what works and what doesn't.

And finally, I revise and test again. Until I reach a final solution.

Answers are rarely black and white when you work in the world of the law. There's a lot of gray area. We work with judges who sometimes say "Yes," and sometimes say "No," and we can't always predict which way it's going to go. When I get a "No" and was expecting a "Yes," my first thought is to try to figure out how to prevent it from happening again.

As a boss myself now, I'm always looking for employees who remind me of me. Who approach work and life the way I do, as fixers. Laziness = Death. You can't be scared to work to achieve success!

Nothing is easy, just work smart. Be the person who steps up when others step back. Look at problems like they're puzzles to be solved instead of mountains that can't be climbed. You need to stay positive and believe in yourself no matter what, manifesting success in your mind for it to happen.

ASK WHY

Rejection and failure are facts of life. Ladysharks recognize them as just another part of the journey. Ladysharks persist in the face of "No" by spending a lot of time asking "Why?"

My mom likes to joke that she waited and waited for me to learn how to talk, but that once I started talking, I never shut up. And of course, my favorite question was "Why?"

My clients often say "No" to important procedures, even when they really need them. It's usually because they're scared or don't have all the facts. One of my clients was in serious pain and needed multiple surgeries. But she absolutely refused to try an epidural and less invasive procedure as an easy fix without surgery.

This made no sense to me. After a lot of prodding, I finally got her to tell me why. Turns out, she'd heard somewhere that steroids make you gain weight, that epidurals include steroids, and therefore the whole thing was a no-go for her. Once I understood why she was saying "No," I was able to help her have a productive conversation with her doctor and find a solution.

When you get a "No," if you don't ask "Why," you'll never know the because. I often find the key is understanding the "No" in the first place.

People sometimes worry that asking "Why?" seems pushy, but it's all about your demeanor. When asking "Why" comes from a place of curiosity, when it's clear you're making an effort to better understand a situation, you'll be surprised how well that question will be received. And the kinds of doors it can open for you.

I get it. We've got to have rules in life, usually for good reasons. But there are almost always exceptions – and you'll never find them if you don't ask "Why?"

"No askie, no gettie!" That's what I always say.

You have to go the extra mile that "normal" people can't or won't. That's what makes a Ladyshark!

BE BRAVE

Listen, the world is full of potential. It's not enough to just pay attention, to keep an eye out for opportunities – Ladysharks have to manifest them. You have to put out to the universe what it is you want and believe in your ability to achieve it. And that takes courage and strength. It is a necessity for your success journey.

Courage makes a big difference in leading a successful life. Lots of people may have what it takes to succeed, but they're afraid to act on it. As a Ladyshark, you have to stand by your convictions even when it's easier to play it safe. Don't allow your fear to keep you on the sidelines. To prevent you from succeeding. To stagnate.

Because stagnation is the enemy of success, and if sharks don't keep swimming they die.

Ultimately, Ladysharks are driven by a combination of personal passion and a clear sense of purpose. Understanding what you want to achieve and why, then totally dedicating yourself to that vision. That kind of dedication stands out. People are drawn to it, motivated by it. And sure, intimidated by it, too. All things a savvy Ladyshark can make work in her favor.

You have to keep your head up regardless of any naysayers. Believe you will have anything and everything you want, as long as you have a plan, stamina and resilience.

STEP 2:

Swim With Other Ladysharks

Ladysharks never stop hustling. They're driven by a mad desire to learn, grow and succeed. And you can't hustle without understanding who you're swimming with. It's like that other popular book says: It all really does come down to "How to Win Friends and Influence People."

My father would say...

Be savvy - Nothing in life is free. Be cautious if someone is giving and not asking for anything in return.

For a Ladyshark that means...

If you're always giving and never getting anything back, you might want to question what's going on. Make sure you're not getting the short end of the stick

I ended up starting my own law firm almost without really planning to during what was one of the worst times in my life.

I'd been working a cushy full-time associate trial attorney job, where the clients seemed to prefer meeting with me rather than my boss. My boss wasn't happy about this, so he let me go.

As you can imagine, I was shocked and devastated. But it turned out to be a blessing in disguise. He'd actually done me a favor, because I was forced to branch out on my own, renting a tiny office for myself.

Unfortunately, that same week, I suffered the sudden loss of my Aunt Tina, my older "twin," who was more of a sister to me than an aunt. A woman who showed me what a Ladyshark could do. Who ran her own salon, while running a coffee shop across the street. Who spent eight years raising funds for the Guardian Brain Foundation by hosting a motorcycle riding charity event called "Ride for a Cure. A woman I still miss every day.

That next Monday, I had to force myself to go into my tiny office to work on the master plan for my new business. Of course, I wanted to stay in bed. But I couldn't. I had to push through the tears while I reached out to every law firm I knew, asking for per diem or trial work they might have for me.

I was proud to be opening my own firm, but I was also really nervous to be on my own. It was like riding a bike with no training wheels for the first time.

As always, I did what I do when I'm freaking out: I called my father for advice.

"Dad, how do I get more business? How do I do this right now?"

"You've got to put yourself out there, Chrissy," he said. "You've got to go to every event you can, shake hands, look people in the eye, and let people know you're open for business. Business will start pouring in. You kidding me? With your smarts? Who's better than you! You'll have clients in no time."

It wasn't quite that easy, but as always, my father was right. What I needed in that moment was a little pep talk, a kick in the ass, and more of his words of wisdom "It's hard, but it's true. No one is going to feel sorry for you. Just keep going."

Truer words were never spoken.

NETWORKING

My top recommendation, the number one way to hustle without spending a ton of money, is by attending networking events. Look for them. If it's in real estate, law, whatever, look and you shall find.

These events give you the chance to learn from other people. They're the easiest way of creating opportunities, generating business, and just getting ahead in any industry. You must put yourself out there. Let your hunger drive you.

Some of you are probably thinking, "But Chrissy, that sounds awful! I hate those things!"

I hear you. Believe it or not, I'm naturally an introvert. I wish I didn't have to network. But it's part of the job. It's how I find clients and referral sources. It's how I grow my business, and it's how I'm among the first to hear about new trends in my industry. It's also how I find new business in unconventional ways.

It's critical to strategically position yourself around others who can open doors for you, send you business, and make introductions. For a Ladyshark, networking isn't just about exchanging business cards; it's about building relationships that have the potential to be mutually beneficial. One hand washes the other, and both the face. You can never think selfishly or you'll never grow.

Like it or not, I'm devoted to networking events – and you need to be, too. Even on those days when I really don't want to go an event, I suck it up. I put a smile on my face, run a brush through my hair, throw on some lip gloss, and head out to meet people. To explore my community. Because every conversation is an opportunity.

HOW TO FIND EVENTS NEAR YOU

The most practical way to find events to attend is to do a Google search. A few conferences will pop up right away. Pretty much every major metropolitan area has conferences about jobs, careers, technology, and so forth happening all the time. Find one that's a fit for you.

You can also check social media. Join a Meet-up or LinkedIn group that's local to you.

Then there's the old-fashioned way: Phone a friend. Or send a group text asking friends and acquaintances to share their ideas.

What about joining a club? Think about joining a Rotary Club, Elks Club, or other business organization in your area.

Finally, you might consider the groups you already have access to, like the alumni association for your high school or college. They usually host events both in-person and virtually.

I encourage you to find networking events full of people doing what you're doing or what you want to be doing. So you can rub elbows with your future self. And don't forget to think about e-cards or business cards. You'll want to have them ready before you go.

WHO TO TALK TO AND HOW

So, now you've found an event. What should you, as a Ladyshark, do when you get there?

First take a minute to read the room. Really stop and think about all the people and information suddenly available to you.

Consider your goals and how the people in that room might be able to help you reach your goals in any number of ways.

A great way to dive in is to seek out people who are more successful than you, more experienced, more comfortable in their networking skin. This will mean stepping outside of your comfort zone, especially at your first event. But it gets easier, I promise.

I do this at networking events all the time. I'll be in a room full of lawyers and I'll look around for the older, likely more experienced people in the room. I'll walk right up to them and use an icebreaker like, "So, are you a doctor or a lawyer?"

Avoid asking, "Do you mind if I ask you a question?" This displays a lack of confidence. And acting confident is a necessity.

Remember: Everyone feels a little uncomfortable at networking events. By introducing yourself and asking questions, you've just made things a lot easier for that person! You've done them a favor. All they have to do is answer your questions, and the conversation will start to flow. Plus people love to talk about themselves!

Hey, I have no idea if the advice they're going to give me is any good. Hell, I don't even know if they're good lawyers. But I've got nothing to lose by picking their brains.

Also, be mindful of and try to avoid "resting bitch face." Ever been told you've got an RBF? Yep, me too. Sometimes someone will ask me what's wrong, and I'll realize that I was just thinking really hard. Clearly, that's not what it looked like to them!

So yeah, I try to remind myself to smile a little more, or at least not to look like I'm plotting world domination – even though I probably am. Not that I'm trying to be fake, either. But think about it for a minute…who are you more likely to start up an interesting conversation with, someone who looks friendly, inviting and approachable? Or someone who looks like a pissed off bitch?

I get it. This can be especially tough when you're a lone ranger, like I was at the beginning. I was a woman at these events by myself, which I didn't enjoy. If at all possible, I would always prefer to network with a colleague, an employee or a friend so we could clean up the room faster and get back to our regularly scheduled activities like work and family.

What do I mean by 'clean up the room," you ask? Cleaning up the room means going up to each person, or as many people as you can, introducing yourself, handing out business cards, trying to make connections, telling them what you do, finding out what they do, and seeing how you might help each other. It takes effort and commitment, but it's worth your time.

You have to take advantage of every conversation you have. Every time you speak to someone new, it's like rolling the dice. It only takes that one good conversation to open the floodgates and let that wave of business opportunities come rushing through.

I will literally stand there taking mental notes as people talk to me because I always learn something. If you keep an open mind, you can apply what you learn from strangers to your own business goals.

Let's say you want to make clothes. Try to get yourself into a networking event where you can meet designers, entrepreneurs, and other established members of the fashion industry. Ask them how they got started, what their biggest regret is, what advice they might have for you. Usually, people are forthcoming with information.

Or maybe you want to be a club owner. Try going to a club you know you already like. Make an effort to rub elbows with the bartenders, the doorman, and maybe, one day, the people who own the club. Get their stories.

Make new friends! If you're a server, find a way to work at an upscale restaurant so you can network on a daily basis. You never know where your next break will come from.

THE COMPETITION: THERE IS NONE

Ask people questions. Listen to their answers. Show your interest. And be on the lookout for opportunities. After all, these people could be your allies one day.

I hate referring to other people in my industry as "the competition." We're all lawyers being lawyers. It's not like we're reinventing the wheel. We all have different ideas, different processes and ways of doing things. And you never know when you might want to adopt some of someone else's practices, refer a case to them, or get a client referred to you from them!

I like to analyze how other people do things:

What do I like?
What do I not like?

I encourage Ladysharks to think this way as you research the "competition" and engage with them. Ask yourself:

Where did they start?
How are they doing it?
What can I do differently? Better?
And what can I learn from the mistakes they've made, so I don't make the same ones?

OFFER TO HELP

People always love being offered help. They really do. Just make sure your offer comes from a sincere place.

After you've been chatting with someone, before you leave, ask them, "Is there anything I can do for you?" See if you can build a relationship by offering to help, instead of just asking them for favors. People will remember you!

They don't usually make requests right away, but they might offer you an example of what you can potentially help them with in the future to nurture a long term business relationship.

The simple phrase, "How can I help?" can change the dynamic of the entire conversation. It's not just you trying to get info from them. It's you offering to support them. This shows then that the relationship won't be one sided.

They'll remember that down the road when you do ask them for a favor, trust me.

FOLLOW UP FAST

Here's the great thing about networking: It isn't just about what happens during the event. It's also about what happens afterwards.

Be sure to collect people's contact info when you're speaking with them. Never ask if they'd mind if you follow up with them in the future. You must be confident that they will want to hear from you, and they will keep you in mind to do future business together! Then grab a business card if they're old school, or get their email address or connect on LinkedIn. You can even ask for their phone number so you can discuss directly how you might be an asset to them.

The next day, send a quick text DM or email to each person you met. "Hey, it's me, Ladyshark! Thanks so much for sharing your wisdom about [your industry] with me last night at the X Event. I will keep you in mind, and hope you do the same!"

OTHER WAYS TO NETWORK

Don't miss networking opportunities that swim right by you every day! I have people coming in and out of my office notarizing documents all the time. These notaries are in the paths of all kinds of interesting people in all kinds of industries who need things notarized. What a great way to connect with people, learn from people, and yep, find unexpected opportunities.

I like to offer free notary service to people coming through our door in order to give them another positive way to remember us. I tell them to keep us in mind in the future, in case they know anyone who has been in an accident or is injured at work. I also let them know that we have real estate agents who can help them buy, sell or rent. Networking my ass off without even leaving my office!

A former boss of mine worked at a dry cleaners when he was a young man. The owner of a big law firm would get his suits cleaned there, so the two of them would regularly chat. One day the lawyer said to him, "Hey, you're a smart kid. You should think about law school!" This was something my former boss had never even considered before. Today, he has his own multimillion dollar law firm.

Let's say you're a bartender, but you're looking to do more. See if there's a way for you to bartend at a place where people who invest go to schmooze. Where you can rub elbows with people who have lots of money. Pick their brains. Ask for advice. Create a growth opportunity for yourself by building your network while you're getting paid! Always think big!

ALWAYS BE LEARNING

You have an incredible opportunity to be a sponge in this lifetime – to soak up all the knowledge you can. So, listen to me, Ladysharks, you must always be learning.

And that doesn't just mean networking.

I also recommend book learning. There are a lot of amazing books out there...like this one! You can listen to podcasts. You can take online classes. I learn a ton for free by watching YouTube videos and listening to finance, real estate and legal influencers.

I've shared a bunch of links at the end of this book to resources that I've found helpful over the years. Keep your mind stocked with fresh knowledge. Be curious about new ideas.

Learning doesn't have to be dry and dull, and it doesn't have to take place in a classroom setting. You don't have to become a walking encyclopedia. But pay attention to the other Ladysharks swimming around who you're trying to emulate.

Always keep this in mind: If they can do it, why can't you? You can! Just believe in yourself, and you *will*!

STEP 3:

Keep Swimming

Everyone is tired these days, right? The modern world is constantly in motion and there are never enough hours in the day. So unless you've inherited a fortune or have already struck it rich, it can all feel pretty exhausting. Ladysharks accept this reality and keep on swimming.

My father would say...

Be wary - Friends can be like snakes. You have to be watchful.

For a Ladyshark that means...

You have to be careful and be mindful of people's intentions. People can be self interested.

If you've seen my Instagram account, you most definitely have seen some photos of me chilling on a beach with my husband, sipping champagne looking like I don't have a care in the world.

You might think, "Damn. Lucky her, no grind needed."

But trust me, luck's got very little to do with it. If I'm on the beach, I earned that trip through nonstop hard work, pushing myself to the verge of burnout – at which point a vacation was a true necessity!

To be a Ladyshark, you've got to be fully committed to putting in crazy hard work – yes, including long hours and little sleep, at least some of the time. Most of the time, in fact. At least at the beginning, when you're in the "building phase" of whatever you're working on.

When I first started my own business, I worked from 8 am to 3 am almost every day. I didn't have the luxury of a myriad of assistants, so I didn't have the luxury of a good rest. I only got that during my occasional weekend getaways, when I was on the verge of exhaustion. I sacrificed a lot, like having a family in my 20s and getting married young – things I had always wanted.

But these days, I'm confident that I made those sacrifices for good reasons. I had a plan, even if the timeline wasn't what I expected it to be. I can now take time to appreciate my journey and how far I've come. As far as I'm concerned, gratitude only attracts more blessings.

Hard work also means sacrificing some of the stuff you love. I've missed so many Ladies Nights with friends over the years, and I am *never* caught up on what everyone else is watching. In fact, I don't even really watch TV. Who's got the time?! I'm too busy chasing my Ladyshark dreams – and my kids, in the downtime that I do have. There will be time to kick back and watch stuff when I'm old. Shows are overrated anyway!

And speaking of a waste of time…Social media apps can be *very* distracting. They can pull you away from what you should be focused on if you're not careful. Consider deleting them from your phone to break yourself of the habit of getting lost in scrolling all day long. Or maybe have a scheduled time in the morning and evening when you allow yourself to check them for a few minutes. Think of all the time you'll give yourself to do a little extra work, planning, or just resting. All things that will make you a stronger Ladyshark!

NEVER GIVE UP

I try to steer clear of talking about religion or politics—too much drama. But here's the thing: I believe that if you work hard, stay honest, and do what you promise, if you throw goodness into the world, then the world will throw it back.

Good karma, basically.

When I became a mom, I realized I really had only two jobs: Keep the kids alive and healthy, and help them become good people in the world.

I can't tell you how many times, as a parent and as a business woman, I've just been like, "F- this. I'm tired. I don't even care anymore. I want to escape for a minute." But of course, I do care. And I know that I can't give up.

If you're a parent, you've been there. The kids have the stomach flu and have been up all night puking their guts out. You've been comforting them while you try to clean up the mess.

Then guess what? You get the bug from them. Now you're the one bent over the toilet. Plus now that the kids are feeling better, they want to eat. They need a bath. You need a bath. Your work needs you, too. WTF!?

Or maybe you're an entrepreneur like me. You have your main gig - mine is the law firm - and a side hustle. Mine is real estate. And more, of course...

I can't tell you how many times I've had a crazy week with multiple court appearances and trials to attend at my day job, when all I want to do is collapse over the weekend and get a massage at the spa. But wouldn't you know, that's the exact weekend when, in my real estate side hustle, the contractor calls to say the new windows aren't arriving on time and there's a massive Nor'easter about to hit and we'd better figure out how to cover those windows up or our freshly refurbished house will be completely destroyed!

No rest, no breaks.

You can be tired, we are only human. But you can't quit. Because then you'll be like everyone else who doesn't accomplish what they're trying to accomplish. You can't give up if you want to succeed.

No one ever said it would be easy. But I promise, it will be worth it.

HOW BAD DO YOU WANT IT?

I never really studied much. For most of high school and college, I just winged it and somehow managed to get by with a last minute looksy at the material before an exam, or pulling an all-nighter writing a paper. Everything was usually OK.

But trust me, that did not work when I got to law school. Not even close!

Law school was the hardest thing I'd ever faced. It truly was like learning a whole new language. It was *hard*. I was tired all the time. And there were lots of times when I just wanted to give up. Again and again, I'd wonder what in the hell I was doing there. How did everyone else do it?

When I felt depressed and lost, I'd call home. My father would say, "Remember why you're there. You're there for a reason. Remember what that reason is." Of course, as usual, he was right!

That's what led me to my mantra, the words that got me through, that made me find more energy deep down:

How bad do you want it?

I wrote those words on a postcard, piece of paper, anything I could find, and taped it to my workstation, my cubicle which I would "move into" for 5-weeks of crunch time each semester, even my bathroom mirror. Every time I wanted to give up, I would say it out loud to boost myself up.

Of course you know that this story has a happy ending. I did it! I graduated from law school, studied my ass off and passed the bar on my first try, thankfully. That was my path to becoming a licensed attorney in the great state of New York.

It's a cliché, but it's true: *If it were easy, everyone would do it.* If you keep finding ways to motivate yourself and put in the work, then it's only a matter of time.

STAY FLEXIBLE

Success rarely comes from doing the same thing over and over again without making changes. You're going to run into obstacles and failures, which may knock you down.

Get back up! A Ladyshark must be resilient. The business world is constantly evolving – and you have to evolve, too.

Remember, you're not the first person to do what you're doing. Other people have been there before you. They've seen it and done it all before. So instead of reinventing the wheel, reinvent the angle that you're looking at the wheel from. Work smart and shape the path to success your own way.

Then again, you can't assume that what you've been doing is going to work forever, or that what someone else did will work for you.

When I first started my law firm, I tried advertising in the newspaper. That worked for a while, but when the world went digital, I tried placing ads on the backs of buses. And while that got me some brand recognition, it was really expensive. So then I moved on to try social media, which was more affordable and allowed me to target a specific audience.

Whether it's advertising tactics or different ways of generating business, you've got to stay agile. Keep checking to see what's working for you and what isn't. Keep track of where your business and referrals come from. Don't just wing it. Believe me, I've tried the "winging it" method, and it doesn't work. Learn from my mistakes so you won't waste time going down the wrong path.

For me, being agile has also meant being as versatile as possible. I have a law firm and a real estate brokerage, among other businesses. I speak fluent Greek and Spanish. When I meet someone new, there are lots of different ways for me to connect with them, be helpful to them, and possibly make money *with* them. Try not to think in terms of making money *from* other people, because it's easy to come across as greedy and selfish. Instead think about how you can work and grow together to generate wealth.

Being adaptable is how you stay relevant. Whether that means learning new skills, adopting a new perspective, or pivoting your whole business model. The key is to never get too comfortable. Don't get complacent. There's always more for you to master.

Ladysharks need to do more than just swim. You've got to be able to run, jump, climb and fly, too!

WORKING HARD MEANS THINKING HARD

I like to say that I'm amazing at improv because my mother beat me as a child. (It always gets people's attention when I say it, that's for sure!)

What I really mean is that when I was in trouble as a little kid, if I didn't have the right answer for my mother within about two seconds, I had exactly one more second to come up with a better one before she whacked me on the butt with a wooden spoon or a flying pandofla (the Greek word for flip-flop). Those were her favorite implements.

Ladysharks have to be quick on our feet no matter what profession we're in, whether we're selling, serving, or just surviving. Otherwise, we'll sink, look incredible, or seem boring.

My father instilled in me at an early age that I could be whatever I wanted to be. He told me, "You've got to work hard. And you've got to work smart, so that you can be the best."

He spent his life doing intense physical labor with his hands, but he wanted me to have more options. So he encouraged me to work hard with my brain. To think hard. In my opinion, you've got to be a critical yet open-minded thinker. Too critical, and you shut doors on yourself. Too relaxed, and you risk being taken advantage of or overlooked.

Here's an example. I had a paralegal I had to let go of right before Christmas. She promised the world and she delivered nada. It sucked having to fire her, but being sentimental doesn't pay the bills or help the rest of my team who are out there pulling their weight. I had to protect my team. I had to think through every aspect of what was going on and make a tough call. I had to keep swimming.

WHAT IS LUCK?

Sometimes people have this misconception that I'm just really lucky – and that bothers me. Because yes, I believe in luck. And yes, I have, in fact, been very fortunate in my life. I was born into a strong, supportive, loving family in a country full of opportunities at a time when a Ladyshark can kick ass and take names.

But if you don't put in the work, luck doesn't mean shit. Looks don't mean shit either.

It's not like I picked a winning lottery number or something. Law felt impossible to me at times. The amount of information I had to retain to make it through law school and become a truly good attorney was massive. Not to mention the seven years of insanity it took to build up my business to where it is today.

Was I lucky it all worked out? Sure. But don't tell me that my success is a matter of luck. I worked really damn hard to create this result. And I fight every day to keep it, because I know it could all be gone in the blink of an eye.

It's a tough world out there. And sure, it's always nice to find a shortcut. But the truth is, the path of a Ladyshark is anything but easy.

In my experience, things that come easily usually aren't worth it anyway.

STEP 4:

Step 4. Dive into the Deep End

Ladysharks aren't afraid to fail because they know that risk is their ticket to big success. They get innovative. They experiment. They take chances swimming in deep water – but only once they've done some due diligence. You need to doggy paddle before you scuba dive. That's how to find opportunities that allow you to get ahead and stay ahead.

My father would say...

Be accountable - You have to keep your word. All you have is your word.

For a Ladyshark that means...

Don't say you're going to do something if you're not going to do it. If you can't keep your word, and you can't produce what you're saying you can produce, you risk being seen as a liar, and a bad business person. You'll never make it to the next level..

I've told you that while I'm a PI lawyer, my side hustle is looking for rundown houses to fix and flip. Here's the thing: 90% of people who tour these crappy old houses just pass at once because the places look like beat up, disheveled dumps to them.

As a Ladyshark, I pause to consider all the angles. Could the house be fixed up without too huge of an investment? Maybe the house isn't worth fixing, but the lot is worth something to a builder or investor I know? What else can I do with this opportunity that others keep passing up?

In 2021, after I had my first daughter, I heard about a tiny old house, an off-the-market property no one saw the value in, so it had remained unsold. It was a 2-bedroom, 1-bathroom place a little over an hour outside of New York City. And even though it didn't look like much, a house like that was almost unheard of for only $240,000 anywhere in New York. It wasn't far from the train station or Home Depot, and there were a bunch of nice supermarkets around.

I was sure I could do something with it. So I bought it in January of 2022.

Boy, did I work some magic...I sold it a year later as an adorable 3-bedroom, 2-bathroom house for $395,000. After the commission and renovation costs, I had earned about $100,000 in less than a year from a side hustle. Not bad, right?

You want to know how I did that? I took a risk *and* I put in the work.

My husband and I showed up every weekend with our 4-month-old daughter in tow. With help from my father, Papa Spiro, we swung sledge hammers to do the demo, found deals on paint, appliances, and fixtures, and teamed up with my father's day laborers who were looking for extra construction work on the weekends. We worked our asses off and it paid off.

Always take into consideration how you might take advantage of what someone else calls "a bad deal" or something with "no margins:" If you're smart about it and willing to take a risk, you might be surprised by what you can do.

TRUST YOUR GUT... SORT OF

New opportunities often come with risk. So do your due diligence. Don't make hasty decisions. Accept that sometimes, you're going to have to just go with your intuition. Follow that sixth sense. (I'll elaborate on that in my next book!)

At the same time, you've got to remember those old sayings "Things aren't always what they seem" and "You can't always judge a book by its cover." Sometimes you're presented with an opportunity that looks like a platter stacked with gold. But when you look closer, the thin layer of gold flakes off, and you're left with a big stack of shit instead.

So while you have to trust your intuition, you also have to make sure you think things through, call on experienced friends, whatever it takes. There are untrustworthy people everywhere you go.

As my Cuban mother-in-law likes to say, "Todo que brilla no es oro." Everything that shines isn't gold. If I had a penny for everyone who's promised me a dream or a "great deal," I'd be rich off of that money alone!

I once had a guy walk into my law firm after getting his mail at the post office on the corner. He asked to speak with an attorney, and so of course I obliged. He showed me a piece of paper from the DMV that said that his car was going to be auctioned at a body shop, something I'd never heard of happening. And his car was really nice, almost brand new, so I took a closer look.

He'd been in an accident, and some random tow truck had showed up right away (presumably after listening to a police scanner). They'd basically grabbed his car, handed him a slip of paper, and taken the car to their shop "to be stored." Then while he was figuring out what to do next, waiting for his attorney to work with the insurance company to pay for the damages, the body shop told him that the storage fees on his car amounted to more than the car was worth. So they were going to auction his car off to get paid for the storage fees on his shiny new Cadillac!

The DMV notice he was holding was literally telling him that his car was going to be auctioned by this body shop. It was some crazy shit, to say the least!

I asked him when he'd found his lawyer. He said he'd been introduced to his lawyer *by the same tow truck people who had taken his car!* This poor guy was caught up in some kind of shady scam. Luckily, he found me to save the day...Super Chrissy to the rescue! I did an emergency order to show cause to stop the car from being auctioned.

So you have to be vigilant, or people will take advantage of you. Like this poor client who'd thought that the tow truck and body shop had come to his rescue.

Generally, I try to give people the benefit of the doubt. But I've been burned many times. I've been lied to, cheated by, and deceived by people I thought I could trust. So part of my success has depended upon my becoming a realist. No matter how much I've wanted to believe that people have good intentions, in my experience, kindness can often be taken as a sign of weakness. While I plan to remain optimistic and giving when I can be, I also always keep an eye out for red flags. It's too easy to find yourself in shark infested waters – and not the good, helpful Ladyshark kind!

Trust me, I'd rather stay the hopeless romantic, you know? I'd rather believe in the basic goodness of others. But it's inevitable that you'll meet some bad sharks as you swim around this ocean of life. You can get stuck in the seaweed of their bullshit if you're not paying close attention.

But you can't let that slow you down. You have to shake the seaweed off and dive back in. Take note of what happened, and try not to make the same mistake twice.

Prepare yourself, Ladyshark. The fact of the matter is, identifying genuine opportunities and separating them from the countless hoaxes, schemes and mirages out there is a skill earned through experience—and a few hard learned lessons.

PRO vs. CON LISTS

Part of identifying true opportunities in life includes dealing with being told "No." I hate the word "No." I always have and I always will. A fact I'm sure my mother can attest to.

In my mind, I'm always looking for ways to overcome the "No." So my first response, as I've mentioned before, is to respond with:

Well, Why?
How come?
What is the reason behind your No?
How can I make it a Yes?

When an opportunity presents itself, I like to make a pro vs. con list.

I love these kinds of lists. When it comes to taking risks, trying new things, and making decisions, I'm obsessed with writing down the pros and cons. It's something I learned from my mother.

Honestly, I think it all started with a boy when I was about 18. I'd been dating this guy for a while, and there were some things I liked about him, like the fact that he was working hard to become a doctor, and my parents really liked him. But there were some things I didn't like, too. Like how he never had time for me, didn't respect what I was into, and used the phrase "obedient" one time too many.

When I shared all of this with my mom, she told me to write down a list of his pros and his cons. And surprise, surprise...the cons side was way longer. Sadly for "doctor-guy," he didn't make the cut.

Of course, it's not always that simple. Sometimes your pro list will win, but you'll realize that you don't actually like what that means. If the cons hold more weight for you in the end, that's okay, too.

Let that be an eye opener for you. Perhaps getting to a "Yes" just requires you to think about things differently, from multiple angles, envisioning the reality of both choices.

CREATE YOUR OWN LUCK

To find success, you have to create your own luck. You can't just sit at home waiting for opportunities to come jump in your lap. You have to go out and find them.

You have to seek out people to talk to in order to broaden your network. You have to really listen when they talk. And you have to always be on the hunt for that detail, that connection, that opportunity others might miss. That might just be your key to success.

When you can, surround yourself with the people you want to be like, people you can learn from. If there are five millionaires in the room, and you want to be a millionaire? Make nice and find a way to hang out with the millionaires and learn something from them.

I saw this question once online: *Would you rather be handed $500,000 cash, or get to have a one-on-one conversation with Jay Z?*

Most people chose the money. That makes sense. $500K liquid is a huge chunk of life changing money if you're small minded.

Not a Ladyshark.

A Ladyshark knows that one conversation with Jay Z could change your life. A chance to truly connect with, learn from, and get an introduction to other power players through Jay Z could end up earning you a lot more than $500,000, while growing your knowledge, networking and wealth opportunities

It's a risk either way, right? You could take that $500,000 and try to invest it well. Hope that it makes you even more money. Or you could pick this unique person's brain, maybe make a friend or two, and possibly even build a relationship that leads to opportunities for a lifetime.

PICK YOUR PEOPLE

I like to apply dating rules to my business relationships because just like in dating, there are some risks you have to take in business, and some trial and error is necessary. You've got to play the odds, like a roll of the dice.

Who do you trust?
Who do you feel comfortable with?

Who does your gut tell you feels right?
Who would you prefer to avoid?
Who do you despise?

Stability has always been one of my primary goals in life, which by default means that lack of stability is one of my biggest fears in life. And other people are unpredictable.

Not only that, but life is a rollercoaster – you're up one day and down the next. That's why it's crucial to have people around me who I can really trust. Those ride-or-die people I can depend upon when times are tough. This happens more often than you think it will, even when you're "up."

It's always easier heading into deep water knowing there's someone around with a lifejacket. (OK, OK…I know. Sharks don't need life jackets. You know what I mean!)

AVOIDING SUCCESS

I'm convinced that one of the main reasons most people aren't rich is because they're terrified of taking risks. Of losing. Of failing. Of embarrassing themselves.

In my experience, if your focus is on avoiding failure, then you're basically also avoiding success.

Let me say that again: If you avoid failure, then you're avoiding success.

Being able to embrace risk is to view it not as a threat, but rather as a gateway to opportunities – *even if you fail.* This is crucial for Ladysharks. Ladysharks are strategic. They always have a plan A, B and ideally, C!

Embracing risk also means seeing beyond whatever immediate challenges present themselves. Recognizing potential where other people see dead ends. Exploring opportunities that other people miss. That's what separates the successful from the spectators.

The ocean of opportunity is vast. It's full of treasures and a few land mines. So trust your instincts while you keep a healthy dose of skepticism on hand. Dive into that deep water to see what's out there. You never know how close you might be to finding the one puzzle piece you need to achieve stability and financial freedom. It could be only a conversation away.

STEP 5:

Be a Relatable Ladyshark

A Ladyshark has to be a people person. Period. Whether you like other people or not, you've got to make peace with the importance of empathy and approach each conversation with a smile on your face. In my experience, people who value empathy do better, go farther, and frankly, are the people I prefer to work with.

My father would say...

Create opportunities - Nothing is easy in life, but you cannot give up.

For a Ladyshark that means...

Be hungry and loyal, because that's what a Ladyshark looks for in others.

I've lived in Queens, on Long Island, and in Brooklyn throughout most of my life. I've rubbed elbows with just about every type of person you can imagine—rich, not-so-rich, living on the streets, and everything in between.

I can say without a doubt, Ladysharks : Life is about what you know, who you know, and where you're trying to go.

There's a deli by my house that I call "The Bougie Deli" because it's ridiculously expensive. I've been going there since law school whenever I want to treat myself. One of the women who works there is, and always has been, so nice to me. She makes the best cinnamon-hazelnut coffee, she always asks how I am, and we end up shooting the shit every time I'm there.

I hadn't even remembered that I'd given her my business card at some point until the day she called me after being in a car accident as an Uber passenger. She'd gotten hurt and her jerk of a boss, who was barely paying her minimum wage, was making her life hell as she dealt with her injury. She was hoping I might give her some advice.

I did better than that. I ended up getting her $800,000, which changed her life. Now she refers other people to me all the time, which is making me money. All because I made friends at "The Bougie Deli!"

The way I see it, a Ladyshark has got to be a chameleon – able to blend with anyone anywhere. You also need to remember that you're not "better than'' anyone else, regardless of money or status. Never let any of that get into your head. Life can change in an instant. You can't afford to be judgmental or closed-minded. You know why? That's a guaranteed way to miss out on opportunities. You've got to be open to everyone. You never know who might throw a golden idea or opportunity your way.

You might be shocked to hear how far small talk can get you. Just by chit-chatting with someone, getting to know and understand them, you might discover something you have in common or an innovative way you can help each other out.

Develop relationships with all kinds of people in all kinds of industries. You scratch their backs, they'll scratch yours. It's a major part of being a relatable person and a great way to be remembered.

READ THE ROOM

Ladysharks need to be aware of how they present themselves to the world. I'm not telling you to change who you are. I'm just reminding you to read the room and adjust yourself accordingly.

At my first personal injury trial, I watched the defense attorney go on and on to the jury we were picking, about how she'd just gotten back from vacation and was really hoping the case would be a quick one so she didn't lose her "relaxed vacation mindset."

I mean, sure. Everyone knows it's nice holding on to that refreshing headspace after you've had a break. But she stood there saying this to people on jury duty! People who did not want to be there. Who were not getting paid more than a few bucks to be there.

I just shook my head, thinking, "Read the room, lady!" I jumped on that jury and won them over easily by pointing it out, saying, "I don't know about y'all, but I sure wish I'd had a vacation this year!" She hadn't read the room, and she'd shot herself in the foot.

Probably won't surprise you to hear that she lost that case to me, huh?

CONFIDENCE IS KEY

Confidence is tricky. Too much of it and you risk coming across as a jerk or cocky. Too little and you can go unnoticed or appear insecure.

And yet the thing is, true, solid, healthy confidence draws people in – especially other people with confidence! I find the key is to balance your confidence with some friendly open-mindedness. Now sit back and watch all that good energy you're putting out into the world come right back to you.

Here's a confession: My confidence is directly impacted by what I wear.

We've all heard it before: *Dress for the job you want, not the one you have.*

My every day go-to is dark or black jeans and a bodysuit with a cute belt. I feel comfortable in that, therefore I feel confident. But I've always got my "lawyer costume," as I call it, handy for when it's showtime. For real. As in, I actually carry a blazer in the back of my car at all times, and I have one hanging in every office I work from.

If I have to hop on a Zoom call with a client or walk into a courtroom at the last minute, at least I can just throw a blazer on! It helps me get into the right mindset and makes me feel ready to take charge.

BE DOWN TO EARTH

Don't forget to couple that confidence with being real. Something I pride myself on is being down to earth.

For me, that means staying grounded in the reality that everyone has a story. I do my best to keep track of more than just work details because I know that each person I work with has a life they're living. They have families, they go on trips, and they have their own opinions about their bosses – just like me. Remembering this helps me connect with people on a human level, and not just as people I'm working with.

So, when I work with a client, I make sure to spend time in every meeting talking to them one human to another, you know? I ask about their kids, their sick parents, summer vacation plans. Heck, we even talk about the weather sometimes.

I really do believe that everyone is equal. If I have skills that can help you, whoever you are, with whatever you need, then let's work together. I try hard never to belittle people. Never to be condescending. I try to be mindful of this in part because I know how shitty it feels to be treated that way.

TAKE A BREATH

When conflict arises, which it always does, take a breath. Try to think before you react – even when you really disagree with the other person. There's not a lot to be gained by losing your cool. You usually lose respect almost immediately.

Taking a breath also helps you slow down, so that you avoid jumping to quick conclusions and making hasty decisions.

To this day, I struggle with being confrontational and not flying off the handle in certain situations. Part of why I became a lawyer in the first place is that I like a good fight. And since both of my parents are confrontational beings, that's how I was raised. That's all I knew. When I was younger, I'd explode if I couldn't confront a situation. It made me feel fake.

But as a business owner, as a boss, I just can't afford to engage in conflict that way anymore, as much as I might naturally want to. I really do take a lot of deep breaths and crack a smile. All the time!

It almost sounds too simple, but it is as easy as thinking before you speak, having some self control, and considering the consequences of your actions.

BE YOURSELF

Don't try to be someone you're not. Try to be even more yourself.

One day when I was in court, I got a call from my office telling me that some Greek guys had shown up there. They didn't really speak English and only wanted to talk to me.

Fine, I was intrigued. I let them know I'd be back in an hour, and they waited for me.

When I walked into my office, I found a tall old man and a short old man standing there. They went on and on in Greek about needing help with their building in Brooklyn, which was being sold on the stock market. Yes, I was confused, too!

Turns out they'd seen my name and photo on a billboard and were convinced that our families came from the same part of Greece. What they were most sure of was that they could trust me, even though I was a complete stranger to them.

Of course, I immediately called my father, who owned some buildings in Brooklyn, too. Fast-forward a few weeks, and my father bought the building from these guys. And he made a great deal.

Why did I tell you this story? Because I've had people laugh at my billboards over the years, even mock me for them. For being my authentic self, 50 feet tall on the side of a freeway. Look who got the last laugh at what happened from my just being myself!

LISTEN UP

Another big part of being relatable is making genuine connections with other people. And to do that, they've got to feel heard.

That means your job is to be a good listener. Ask lots of questions, and really listen to their answers.

Sometimes even when you think you know where a conversation is going, it heads in a new direction. If you're not paying attention, the other person will notice.

Pay special attention to cues other people drop when you're talking. If they talk a certain way, try to adapt to make them feel comfortable, whether that means mimicking some of their vocabulary, or simply slowing down how fast you talk to them.

Another way to show you're listening is to take people up on what they offer you. If someone says they'd be happy to meet up for coffee, take them at their word and assume they actually *would* be happy to meet up for coffee. Send a follow-up note the next day suggesting a time and place. It shows them you were paying attention, and that you know how to take the initiative.

And speaking of following up, it's really important to do it! Follow up with people, don't wait for them to follow up with you. We live in a busy world. Things fall through the cracks for everybody.

If you haven't heard back from someone who you're really hoping to connect with, as long as you're polite about it, don't hesitate to send a follow up email or text. Business communication doesn't obey the "wait three days" rule like dating does (which I think is a bullshit rule, by the way)! If you want something, go get it!

BE SUPPORTIVE

As I've mentioned, I'm a hard worker. I've always been a good employee. But I've had a lot of shitty bosses in my day, and was rarely, if ever, appreciated. So for a long time, I was under the impression that all bosses sucked.

In my 20s, I used to joke with my friends that bosses must go to Boss School to learn how to be assholes with no empathy.

When you're first starting out as a lawyer, it's not uncommon for bosses to want to read over your paperwork before it's filed with the court. No biggie. I've got no problem with that. But I had this one boss who read a motion of mine, then told me to my face that I wrote like shit. He prefaced it with, "No offense," then proceeded to ask me if I thought in Greek or English while I was writing. He said, "The way you're explaining things, it doesn't sound like you're thinking in the English language."

I was offended.
First of all, I was born in America and English is my first language. I do also happen to be fluent in Greek and Spanish. Second, I'd been commended by previous employers, on multiple occasions, on the quality of my writing skills. Third, and most importantly, how shitty could my writing be given my stellar record of winning motions?

Although I was definitely offended by this boss, I refused to let his remarks hurt my feelings. Was he trying to make me feel insecure? Was he trying to boost his own ego? Did he want me to quit working for him? Or was he just a shitty boss? I've got a theory, but I'll let you make up your own mind.

What I will say is that his behavior was the opposite of encouragement or empowerment. I kept that in mind when I started my own business and became a boss myself.

There are so many amazing people out there who work for asshole bosses – nasty people who don't give a shit about them, don't give them bonuses or yearly raises. Like I said, I've worked for a few of them.

Now that I'm a boss, it's important to me to regularly tell the people who work for me that I appreciate them. To make sure they feel wanted, that they feel heard. And that they know their hard work doesn't go unnoticed.

Even though running my own business is a lot harder and more stressful than I could have imagined, even though it always feels like there is so much going on, so much at stake, and even though I feel responsible at all times for every one of my clients and for every one of my employees and their families, I strive to be the kind of boss people *want* to work for.

It has been clear to me from the get-go that if I want my business to succeed, I need great employees who want to work with me. So I need to do everything I can to support them. And so should you – whether you're an employee or an employer. Don't settle for less.

BE LOYAL

One of my top goals as a boss is to surround myself with loyal people. I believe loyalty is built by ensuring that people feel valued and appreciated.

I tell the people who work for me, "If you need me, call me. I'll be there for you, whether it's personal or business!" And I mean it.

I never had a boss say anything like that to me. I never felt much loyalty from any of them, despite being a loyal employee who often worked closer to 80 hours a week than 40. I want my employees' experience to be different, to be full of long-term career vibes instead.

That said, while we can agree that nobody wants to work for a "bosszilla," if you're too nice, you risk people taking advantage of you. I don't want employees who are just in it for the paycheck, clock-watching instead of being team players.

I want loyal Ladysharks. I want employees who are hungry, who are willing to put in the work, who want to further their careers, who enjoy what they do, and who enjoy working with me to grow the company. Those are the employees who I am loyal to in return.

Remember, a relatable Ladyshark is an unstoppable force. You never know who's going to be your next client, your next connection, your next big opportunity. Your boss today could be your client tomorrow. So, be friendly, be authentic, be confident…and watch the whole ocean open right up for you.

STEP 6:

Be Prepared AF

I'm all about planning for the storm. Not because I'm a pessimist, I look at the glass half full. But I like to feel like I'm a few steps ahead of the game. Try to organize a safety net around yourself as you Ladyshark your way through life. Think proactively, not reactively.

My father would say...
Be aware: Happiness brings friends, difficulties test them..

For a Ladyshark that means...
Everyone wants to be around someone when they're up, but when you're struggling, it's a test of who will stick around. Some people will take your kindness for weakness. Don't let other people take advantage of you.

Start your day with a cup of coffee and a chat with yourself where you ask, "What wrench could life possibly throw at my plans today?"

And then, boom, you're brainstorming ways to dodge those wrenches should they happen to come. You're already ahead of the game, and you haven't even stepped into the office yet.

I do a lot of test, check, revise—rinse and repeat. And that's not just for work stuff; it's for life stuff, too. Especially when it comes to interacting with other people.

The next time you're headed into a meeting with someone you've met before, take a quick minute to think about how things went the last time you talked. Ask yourself:

What worked with this person?
What didn't?
What kind of tweaks can I make to ensure this next conversation is more successful?

And make sure you remember names. When you meet someone, repeat their name. When you see them again, use their name. Everyone loves to hear their name, and you'll be earning points with them every time you do it!

KEEP IT IN BOXES OR ON LISTS

Life can get really messy. Something I rely on to get me through the messier times is compartmentalizing. I mean, hey, most of us keep our socks in one drawer and our shirts in another, right? It just makes sense.

One thing I do to help keep things organized is to make to-do lists for everything. Literally everything. I have my law work list. My real estate list. My children list. My husband list. And a bunch of other lists, too! (I even had a big list dedicated just to making this book happen.)

Just like Santa, I make my lists and check them twice (or more like 50 times), because what good is a list if you're not making your way through it to get things done?

And in those moments when the pressure of having all these things on all these lists starts to weigh down on me? When the anxiety about what the sum total of what is on all these lists starts to feel like too much? What do I do then?

Tackle one thing at a time, by order of importance. Pay attention to deadlines. And breathe.

It's not a problem, until it's a problem.

Ladysharks are problem solvers, so we'll fix it.

It's all about perspective. Yes, I'm closing on a house today, the oil light is on in my car, my kids kept me up all night, and I'm due in court in five minutes. I'm tired and I'm overwhelmed. But you know what? It could always be worse. You have to be thankful for being so busy…The alternative will never give you fulfillment or bring you success.

Everyone has problems. Everyone's life is complicated. Most of us are tired and overwhelmed for our own set of reasons. Don't fool yourself into thinking otherwise.

Now, stand up straight, take a deep breath, and believe that tomorrow will be a better day. And don't forget to use those lists!

BE READY TO POUNCE

For Ladysharks, being prepared means being ready to jump on opportunities at any time, in any place.

I was getting my eyelashes done the other day. And obviously, your eyes have to be closed when that happens, you know? You can't do shit. You can't text. You can't even really talk. So I was just lying there listening, happy to get an hour-long break from my phone, from damage control at work, and from screaming babies (LOL).

The woman next to me was getting her lashes done, too. She was talking about how she works for an architectural firm, and how they go to colleges to recruit graduating architects. Meanwhile, in my head, I'm hearing all kinds of possibilities.

So I just jump right in there, eyes closed, no idea what this lady looks like, and I say, "I'm so sorry. I don't mean to eavesdrop, but I heard you talking, and my nephew is actually in college for architecture. He's really smart and good at what he does!"

"Oh, really?" the lady says. "Where does he go to school?"

"He's a junior at Syracuse," I tell her.

"That's great," she responds. "We definitely recruit from there."

So I ask her for her contact info to pass along to my nephew. Then I say, "Listen, I'm an attorney. If you ever need anything, call me. I'll give you my card when I can open my eyes."

Just like that, I may have gotten my nephew a job, and I've got a new person who could one day become a client or send me one. And I did it all with my eyes closed!

Always be ready to pounce!

SO MUCH TO TRACK

We've all got our Achilles' heel. For me, it's keeping all my ducks in a row. Believe it or not, I struggle to stay organized. It's something I'm always trying to get better at. And we live in a crazy, fast-paced world, so staying organized isn't just a nice goal for a Ladyshark—it's essential.

First things first. Write stuff down. Then be sure you have a system so that you can find what you wrote down. Even if you've got a memory like an elephant, things will slip through the cracks. It's inevitable.

So whether you're a notebook jotter, a daily-planner devotee, or you've gotten really good with the apps on your phone, make time to develop a system that works for you. Find a way to keep yourself from misplacing the name or number of that one person you met that one day who may very well have been the key to you making millions...if only you could find their information.

And remember, life's a juggling act for all of us. Between family birthdays, work deadlines, no school days, travel, and oh yeah, your own sanity, it's a lot of balls to have in the air at once.

If you don't keep track for yourself, nobody else will. And that's a recipe for disaster.

BE ORGANIZED

To reiterate: being organized isn't just a skill, it's a secret weapon. I don't think you can be truly successful without it.

Yet it's something I wrestle with on a daily basis. I like to think of being completely organized as a destination – somewhere I'm always heading, but probably won't ever actually reach 100%. That's OK, though, because along the way, I'm experimenting and learning and failing and trying again, all with that destination in mind.

Organization touches every aspect of our lives: paying bills, crafting business plans, dealing with clients, you name it. Without it, you're basically trying to sail a ship without a compass. Spoiler alert: it doesn't end well.

So take stock of what's messy in your life, what could benefit from a reorganization. For instance, if your work space is a disaster, your brain is probably not far off. How are you supposed to crush it in life if you're living in chaos? A messy desk means a messy mind.

Ladysharks, being prepared is power. It means you're not just surviving life's storms, you're navigating them like a bad-ass. Organize your thoughts, your information, and your life. That's how you'll stay a few steps ahead.

CHILL OUT

Don't be confused when I tell you to be ready, get organized, stay on top of everything… and then tell you to chill out. That's part of being prepared, too. You've got to know when to panic and when not to panic.

Whenever I get worked up about things going wrong, my father says to me, "But did you kill someone?"

To which, fortunately, I am always able to say, "Well, no." (Thank God.)

"Then everything will be fine," he promises me. "You'll figure it out."

And he's right, I always do.

Having a law firm with thousands of clients, something "bad" happens on a daily basis. The word "bad" becomes kind of relative when you're dealing with bad shit all day, every day. It's damage control every day, there are just different levels of it. You can panic, or you can chill out and figure out how to fix one thing at a time.

TAKE CARE OF YOURSELF

People always talk about how important it is to take care of our bodies. And of course, that's true. But don't forget to take care of your mind, too. This is yet another part of being prepared.

A Ladyshark has to be able to think clearly. Otherwise you're likely to miss out on all kinds of opportunities. You do need a basic amount of sleep and some self care.

You can only be knee deep in the daily grind, burning the candle at both ends, for so long before you burn out. And then what good are you? Nervous breakdown? Depression? Don't let yourself get to this point. Pay attention to your body, and try to give it what it needs. This means building in some downtime for both your body and your brain.

True power lies not in impulsiveness, but in thoughtful action. Take calculated risks. Choose your battles wisely, keep your shit together, and focus on progress, not perfection. One foot in front of the other.

STEP 7:

Show Yourself Some Respect

Ladysharks: The sooner you can learn how to respect yourself, the stronger you are going to be! This is how you will dominate in business. This is how you will accumulate wealth to pass on to future generations. This is how you will find true love. Take it from someone who's been lost in the deep sea trenches and had to struggle to paddle her way out.

My father would say...

Be smart. You can't work 9-5 and then go sit on the couch. You'll never make money like that..

For a Ladyshark that means...

Be able to hold your head up high and have a clear conscience about how you do business.

I've always been a really bad test taker. Tests bring on a lot of anxiety for me. I didn't do well on my SATs. It's a miracle I even got into law school given how anxious I was about taking the LSAT. But somehow I made it through, and I was proud!

Then I got to law school. Turned out the exams were much harder than I ever could have anticipated. My brain would just shut down in the middle of them. I would have full-blown panic attacks.

Literally, I'd sit down to take an exam and everything would go fuzzy. I'd start the exam sometimes, and then all of a sudden the teacher would be calling "Time!" I'd be thinking, "What the hell just happened?!" My brain would completely check out on me. It was scary. I'd never felt out of control like that before.

I ended up having to meet with the registrar because my grades were slipping as a result of this test-taking anxiety. Let's be clear: I went to a law school where one out of every three people fail out, and I was trying desperately not to appear on the losing side of those statistics.

All I can say is: Bless. That. Registrar! That gentle, middle-aged woman was so generous with me. She showed me empathy and gave me the advice I desperately needed exactly when I needed it. And thank God she did. She saved me.

"You know, my husband is an attorney, and he dealt with the exact same problem when it came to taking tests during law school," she said.

"How did he make it to graduation?" I asked.

"He found a hypnotherapist! You should give it a try," she explained with an encouraging smile.

Of course, my first thought was of those ridiculous episodes of the Maury Pauvich Show or the Jerry Springer Show, where they hypnotize people and then parade them out on stage meowing and barking.

No way was I doing that!

But I was also desperate. So I kept an open mind and did my research. And although I was still skeptical, I went with it, thinking, "What do I have to lose?!" Because not doing something was not an option.

I ended up finding what seemed like a reputable doctor whose office was not far from my law school. He was a tall, thin man with kind eyes and a supportive smile.

On my first visit, when I expressed my fears and skepticism, he explained how hypnotherapy was all about connecting to your subconscious being.

"You won't be clucking around my office like a chicken or something during our sessions!" he reassured me. "We'll spend our time helping your subconscious accept that when your body wants to panic, it does not have to panic. Your mind can help your body manage the panic. Also, you must eat almonds."

"Why almonds?" I asked him, instantly suspicious.

"First," he said, "because cutting back on sugar in times of anxiety can be helpful." Then he went on to explain how he'd help me reprogram my subconscious to use the ritual of eating almonds to trigger my body into calming down so I could perform well during an exam.

If I'm being perfectly honest with you, I thought he was probably full of shit. But I tried it anyway. That's how desperate I was.

And I swear to God, it worked! I still had test-taking anxiety, but I was no longer experiencing the same kind of total shut-down panic attack.

After a few sessions with him, when it came time for my next exam, I was able to function. Slowly munching one almond after another, I was able to breathe, relax, and focus just enough to tame my anxiety and not fail another exam.

I'm not saying hypnotherapy turned me from a D student to an A student. But I was able to stay in the world of Bs and Cs, which was good enough for me. I knew that I understood the material backwards and forwards, I was only struggling to put it on paper at exam time.

I am absolutely certain I wouldn't have made it through law school without this help. Without respecting myself and my struggle with anxiety enough to do something about it.

And this experience is what led me to the fantastic world of guided meditations, which I'm now devoted to.

GUIDED MEDITATIONS

The hypnotherapy helped me with taking tests, but like lots of people, I struggle with anxiety in multiple aspects of my life. With all the drama that comes with being a lawyer, juggling multiple businesses, and raising a young family, how could I not?

Fortunately, like so many others, I've discovered the world of guided meditations on YouTube. Listening to them at night before bed really helps me out. Sometimes I listen to calming ones that help me wind down after a stressful day. And sometimes I listen with very specific learning goals in mind.

Initially, I spent time learning about organizational skills (something I wanted more of), procrastination (something I wanted less of), and attracting wealth (something I always wanted!)

A few years ago, I sought out meditations about attracting an incredible romantic partner. I was ready to build a life with someone, and with my crazy work schedule, I didn't even know how to start.

Say what you will about manifesting things, guided meditation, positive thinking, prayers…all I know is that in less than a year, I had met my now husband. He is very much the incredible partner I'd been looking for. Of course no relationship is perfect. You're always going to have some disagreements and differences of opinion. The key for me has been approaching my marriage with loyalty, empathy and respect.

I promise you there's something for everyone out there, and you really can explore meditations for almost any aspect of life. In the middle of the night when I can't sleep, I put on a guided meditation. It works just like hypnotherapy did for me, tapping into something deep in my subconscious that helps me chill the hell out. At least enough to doze off.

And I'll never forget a specific guided meditation I listened to about attracting wealth. It was all about boulders. It talked about how debt is like a boulder, and how spending money on a credit card adds to that boulder, making it heavier and heavier. To this day, I picture a boulder every time I use my credit card, which helps me keep an eye on my purchasing habits and splurges.

Before I started listening to guided meditations, I was a master procrastinator. Because I work well under pressure, I was always putting things off and having to scramble to get them done last minute. Honestly, it was a pretty exhausting way to work. You can't really be successful if you're a procrastinator. It's just not sustainable. You'll burn out.

The guided meditation I discovered provided me with ideas and inspiration for how to tackle something I really struggled with… even while I was half asleep. And I kid you not, I don't procrastinate anymore!

If it's not clear yet, I'm a *huge* fan of getting out of your own head and being guided through your thoughts by someone else every once in a while. If you're interested in giving it a try, I've linked to some of my favorite guided meditations on the book website: **www.theladyshark.com**

SOCIAL MEDIA

Ladysharks want to leave a big impression. Ladysharks want to stand out from the crowd. And that's certainly always been part of my personality. It has always been vital to me that I get to be me. But sometimes that means posting a picture of myself that, let's say, my mother isn't so happy about.

It can be really hard not to take things personally when it comes to social media. I actually heard someone say this about me once, "Sure, she's good looking. And OK, she's got a lot of clients. But look at her social media. Look at what she's posting." It didn't feel good to hear. I mean, who the hell wants to hear something like that?

But what can I do? Just keep on being me. Everyone has an opinion. Who cares!?

Whether we like it or not, a lot of times, life is a popularity contest. The way I look at it is, if someone sees something I post and I get a job out of it…Great! If that happens to be thanks to what I look like? Great! If it's because I'm a good lawyer? Great! I'm growing. I'm getting jobs, one way or another. I'm providing for my family.

And I'm being true to myself.

Do I push the line sometimes? Sure. I've posted photos of myself in a bikini. I don't see anything wrong with that. I know the difference between what I post on social media and who I am as a person with my friends and family. I know the difference, even if everybody else doesn't. And it's not my job to teach them!

YOU'RE IN CHARGE

Sometimes when people meet me in real life, they seem surprised that I'm not an idiot. That I'm pretty damn smart, on point, and good at what I do.

Blame the dumb blonde stereotype, I guess. Blame the bias against my outer shell, the curves, my Queens attitude, my big hair and my fearless fashion.

I used to be offended by what other people thought of me, but you know what? Now I just own it. I can't control what other people think. All I can do is be myself. Unapologetically.

Here's what I will say: If you're going to wind up embarrassed about doing something, don't do it. If you don't want people to find out about something, don't do it in the first place. Especially in this day and age, where tech reveals all. The truth almost always comes out.

Chances are, if you do something really crazy, remotely offensive or over the top, people are likely to find out. That's just the way our world works these days, you know? So when it comes to social media, if you're going to post a photo of yourself, then be sure you're not embarrassed about that photo in the first place.

I believe in total transparency. I stand by what I post as part of respecting myself. At least you know exactly what you're getting with me! Not everybody likes it, but I go to bed at night respecting myself and my choices.

So remember, it's your social media account and your life. You're the one choosing what to post. You can't control how people are going to respond or what they're going to say. As you know, it won't always be nice things. But you chose to do it. So you have to accept their reactions and stand by your decision.

The world is not always a pretty place, Ladysharks. You have to have thick skin and roll with the fact that you can't make all the people like you all the time.

WHOSE FAULT IS IT?

I hate bad reviews. They drive me crazy. They make me want to scream and cry, because there is really nothing you can do to make them go away. But in my business, like a lot of other ones, they simply come with the territory.

How do I deal with them? How do I process that kind of public criticism? My parents raised me with a strong sense of accountability. The way they put it was, "It's always your fault, even if it's not your fault."

I still think about that all the time, especially when it comes to bad reviews. I do the best job I can for my clients. I respect my own work. So, when I get a bad review, I ask myself:

What can I learn from this?
How could I have prevented this?

What can I do differently to make sure this doesn't happen again? Is this something that's even in my control?

You know what else it means if it's always your fault, even when it's not your fault? It means you should never use the phrase, "It's not my fault." I hate it when other people say that to me, and I don't believe it's a phrase Ladysharks should use. Ever.

When someone in my office makes a mistake on a case, whether it was me, or an associate, or a paralegal, or whoever, I'm the one who falls on the sword. It's the whole, "The buck stops here" thing. I'm the boss.

I'm the one who calls the client, levels with them about what's going on, tells them what we're doing to make it better, and assures them it won't happen again. Sometimes I'll even give them my direct number to show them how committed I am to making things right.

Mistakes happen. The blame game is a waste of time. Take responsibility for yourself and your actions. Be accountable. People will respect you for it, and you'll respect yourself more.

GENEROSITY

In this crazy world we live in, it's easy to get caught up in your own shit. You have bills to pay, loved ones to care for, fires to put out. Hell, sometimes it's a struggle just getting through the day.

Taking the time to help other people can be hard to prioritize, especially when it feels like you're barely taking care of yourself.

But if you can help a friend in need, do it. If you can loan someone a bit of money to get through the month, or find a few minutes to help them move a couch, or even just send a "checking in" text once in a while, do it. You know why? Because one day, you'll be the friend in need.

Having a clear conscience, setting good intentions, and being mindful might sound like new-agey ideas that have no business being part of the business world. But as far as I'm concerned, they're essential elements of being a successful human, and therefore of being a Ladyshark.

ENLIGHTENMENT

I don't really talk about religion all that much because it's not something everyone is comfortable with. I was raised in the Greek Orthodox church, so that's where I was taught about religion. I'd go to church like I was supposed to. And I'd pray like I was supposed to. But it was never personal for me. I never felt like I learned about myself.

As I've gotten older, I've sought out ways to address that, to try to find what works for me spiritually, what might help me to understand myself and life better. I always strive to be my better self. And now, I like to think that I'm growing spiritually strong, or at least stronger.

As I've looked for answers, I've uncovered a lot about myself by examining the obstacles I've faced, exploring what might be coming my way, and deciding how I want to handle the hard stuff. I guess I think of it as seeking enlightenment, and it comes from a place of wanting to respect myself spiritually.

In Greek culture, there's a prayer that you say in order to take away the evil eye – which, as far as I'm concerned, refers to all the negative energy in the world. Whenever I have a problem, I imagine speaking with my godfathers and godmothers, those who came before me, and for whom I have great respect. I try to have faith that they are on my team, looking out for me as I make my way through the world.

Respecting yourself isn't a passive activity. You have to own your voice, stand up for what you believe, and be fully accountable for yourself. Don't let anyone dim your light or silence your roar. The world needs your authenticity, your strength, and your unwavering self-belief.

STEP 8:

Build That Treasure Chest

Most people miss out on generating wealth because they don't know how to recognize a good financial opportunity – even if it's right in front of them. It's not just about stumbling upon a golden ticket or winning the lottery. There are some basic financial skills every Ladyshark should know and put to use.

My father would say...

Respect yourself. Have a clean face..

For a Ladyshark that means...

Find a side hustle, a job that offers bonuses or a way to invest in something that can keep on making you money. You must do this to change your life, even if it's temporary. Doing the same thing and expecting something different is pure madness.

For a lot of people whose goal is financial freedom, the million-dollar question is, "How do I even start?" Making the decision to start at all is an amazing first step! Don't be discouraged. It will happen. But I'll be honest: You'll start by making a lot of mistakes. The good news is, making mistakes is the best way to learn. You're not perfect. Who is?

Ladysharks have to make the most of your mistakes. And not just your own. Pay attention to other people's mistakes, too, so you don't make them yourself.

How?

Read memoirs. Listen to podcasts. Watch YouTube videos. Follow influencers.

Ask tons of questions at networking events and even at family reunions. Learn the histories of successful people you encounter or admire. They're usually full of story after story of all the mistakes they have made along the way.

Even Taylor Swift makes mistakes. (She's my Goddaughter's favorite!) Yep, one of the most powerful, wealthy, successful women in the media and public eye today.

When she was first getting started in the music industry, she signed with a record label and trusted the person running it with control of her master recordings.

Well, that turned out to be a big mistake!

In 2019, the guy sold her entire music catalog to Scooter Braun, a music manager Taylor had a long history of conflict with. She was enraged. She felt betrayed. Allegedly, she even wrote a song or two about it.

But did Ladyshark Taylor let that betrayal stop her? No she didn't. She made a really smart business decision. She chose to re-record her albums, releasing them one by one as "Taylor's Version." Now she owns all that music outright, and she's left her mistake in the past.

That is one bad-ass Ladyshark move right there.

TIME TO BUDGET

The first basic step beyond realizing you'll make mistakes is learning to budget.

How did I learn how to budget?

Well, I've always loved sneakers. When I was growing up in Queens, the fashion was all about sneakers. It defined you. Declared your status. You *had* to have at least one nice pair of sneakers. End of story.

In my family, my brother and I each got one new pair of sneakers in September for back to school. That was it. My parents were not into luxury things. They didn't buy fancy stuff. Hated the idea of showing off. They wanted us to focus on school, not fashion.

So they gave us clothes each fall, but not exactly what we wanted.

Now I have <u>always</u> loved clothes and shoes, so my only option was to earn the money to buy what I wanted by myself.

So, at 14 years old, I got my first job as a cashier at a ShopRite supermarket. I did this to make sure I'd have the money to buy the sneakers I so desperately "needed." Then I budgeted every paycheck, carefully setting aside money for my dream shoes while also growing my savings for a "rainy day."

My parents insisted that 2/3 of my paycheck go into savings. But I got to use the other 1/3 on whatever I wanted. Which was honestly just sneakers and clothes for years!

That 2/3 to 1/3 ratio worked well for me, even though I really wanted to spend 100% of what I'd earned. But it's how I learned not to use all of my money on unnecessary purchases. Try it!

Here's a basic crash course in the art of budgeting. Budgeting *is* an art, something that must be mastered.

Let's start with the most important part: You have to spend less than you make. It sounds simple, but it's difficult for so many people and it's profoundly effective! Resist the urge to splurge on every whim.

Don't get overwhelmed. You can start small. Ask yourself things like:

Do I really need another drink from Starbucks?
Could I bring lunch from home instead of always going out or getting food delivered?
What could I do with that little bit of money if I saved it for a month instead?

It will also likely mean: No Uber Eats. No Instacart. No Amazon. No TikTok Shop. All of these apps are bad news for someone trying to budget. (Don't forget about that boulder credit card story I told you…Every time you buy something that's not a necessity, think of that boulder weighing even more!)

I am mindful of every dollar I spend. And I love a good coupon, you know? Finding a deal? I'm a promo code junkie! I don't think you can ever have enough money *not* to try to save money. Have you tried Rakutan? It's a great way to get a percentage off, by way of cash back, on websites you're already shopping on.

Also, don't buy stuff to impress anyone else, "to keep up with the Joneses." Because many of said "Joneses" are living unhappy lives, which you don't see behind the social media lies. It's usually all a hoax!

Don't buy stuff because you think it's going to make you happy, either. Stuff rarely does. At the end of the day, the feeling of being financially stable is worth so much more than the short term gratification of retail therapy. Work hard enough and you'll earn enough to buy whatever you want: a house, cars, and maybe even a rental property.

And make sure to track your expenses diligently. Keep receipts and review your bank statements. Try not to use cash because it's the hardest to keep track of. If you don't know where the money is going, you don't stand a chance at saving it up.

And speaking of saving...

BOTH SIDES OF SAVING

Save for the unexpected. It's called a rainy day fund, but you never know when you might need it mid-summer. Sure, it can be really tough to put aside money to save when you're barely getting by to begin with. But try changing your mindset. This is the number one thing you can do to make a financial change in your life!

Put a dollar or two that you get back as change in an envelope. It doesn't have to be something fancy or formal. You just try to put a few dollars aside each day. If you commit to this baby step every day, your savings will grow. That's how it works. It's inevitable. Once you can commit to $10 a day, do it. Same with $20. You'll have a pile of money to invest before you know it.

That being said, be careful about putting money in the bank and just leaving it there. Once you've saved enough money to start investing, make a plan for how to invest it. Don't limit your growth potential. You have to make your money work for you.

Money sitting in a savings account earning almost no interest does you no good. Use your mind and your drive, and always be on the lookout for investment opportunities, innovative ways to make your money grow.

FROM SAVING TO INVESTING

Once I graduated from high school, my father said, "Enough with the shopping already, Chrissy!" He taught me that investing in something was better than just saving money to buy something disposable that I wanted.

He talked to me about how people so often get tempted by short-term gratification: shopping, fancy dinners, a $10 coffee instead of a $2 coffee, etc. He said, "If you don't have discipline, you'll just end up stuck in the same place. People who want what they want and simply buy it without discipline, usually on a credit card, will never find stability."

And I get it. Who doesn't want a nice car? Nice shoes? A fancy purse, right? But if you can't afford those things, if you're trying to save, where does buying them leave you? In debt, with the same ol' job, paying you the same ol' paycheck, and you with no way of getting ahead or creating extra income for a more comfortable future.

Ladysharks save their money to invest so that they can make more money. So why not find a side hustle? Maybe generate some extra income? Start putting together the money you need to open your own business? That way, you'll be able to buy the car, the shoes, the purse and a whole lot more.

SIDE HUSTLES

Here's a little story about my dad. When he arrived in America at 17, he sought work, got lucky and was hired as a day laborer doing construction. And whenever he could, he did little side jobs for one of his bosses to make some extra money.

One day, after a few years of working hard and proving himself as a trustworthy employee, his boss gave him an old truck he wasn't using as payment for a side job my father had finished up early. (Like a hard working Ladyshark does!) That truck allowed my father to take on even more side jobs in the evenings and on weekends, making it possible for him to save as he worked.

He did this for 9 years before starting his own construction company. Times are a little different now, and 9 years might seem like an eternity, but stick with me…

Around this time, my dad was in a really bad motorcycle accident. One day, when he was driving right past a church, he was hit head on by a drunk driver. His helmet flew off, and he went face first into the concrete, knocking out all his teeth. He was in a coma for three days.

The only reason he lived was that there happened to be an ambulance right behind him when the accident took place. (Well, that and the church, if you're a believer. When my father woke up, he vowed that he would have any children he might have one day christened in that church. My brother and I both were!)

The silver lining to this story is that eventually there was a lawsuit and a settlement. My father received enough money to make his first meaningful investment. He bought an old apartment building in a really rough neighborhood, where he had to take a weapon with him to collect rent in order to make sure he didn't get robbed. But using his construction skills, he was able to fix the building up a little bit at a time. Eventually, he sold it for quite a bit more than he had paid. And he's been buying buildings ever since.

SIDE HUSTLE IDEAS

There are lots of side hustles out there, lots of ways to invest and grow your money, especially now that people can do remote work online. There are tons of online opportunities to make extra income, like leaving reviews, translating documents, taking surveys, and doing customer service.

Or maybe you like to make gift baskets or cheese boards or other DIY things. Why not make something to sell on Etsy? Or even Amazon?

Are you into the whole balloon decorating craze? Why not try event decorating on the weekends?

Or what about buying an ATM? Did you know that anyone can do that? You can buy an ATM. Then you get a fee each time someone uses it, and boom, you're making money. Same thing with vending machines.

Think long and hard about the kind of side hustle that might work for you. A second source of income can help you take another step along the path to financial freedom.

BUYING A BUSINESS

Maybe you're not in side hustle mode right now. Maybe you're more interested in figuring out how to buy a business? It's really not as hard or as expensive as you might think.

Here are some Ladyshark tips for what you should be on the lookout for if you want to buy a business. Look for one or more of these:

- A business that needs an upgrade - because there are still lots of old school businesses with outdated websites, no social media, some even still use fax machines. That leaves a lot of room for you to bring in innovations to pump up the margins.
- A business that is reasonably priced - because every penny counts, and ideally a business with the potential for growth - because you're going to want to use that money you saved on the price to make your business bigger and better.

- A profitable business with a solid history that's proven it can make you money - because there's something called The Lindy Effect that says the longer a business has been around, the better the chances it's going to stick around. Older, established businesses can be hidden gems, and they can often be lower risk. Since you're just getting started, you may not want to risk a lot right out of the gate.
- A business that is understandable - because you don't want to have to go and get a degree in order to figure out how the business works. The most simple business models are the easiest to run. You might consider something like a dry cleaners, a car wash, or a pet grooming business.
- A business with seller financing. What does that mean? It's when there's a loan from the seller to the buyer to help pay for the purchase. Because not everyone has a big stack of money lying around to buy a business. Here's how you could make this work for you:
    - Let's say your local corner deli (bodega) is for sale for $100,000, and you've gotten to know the owner over the years.
    - And let's say a Ladyshark like you, who's got their shit together, is looking for a way to become a business owner.
    - You might only have $2000 right now, but the owner tells you if you can scrape together $10,000, they'll give you a loan for the other $90,000.
    - Then every month, after you pay your rent, you pay the owner $5000.
    - Little by little, you pay the owner back and all your dreams will come true because you own the store yourself.

- And finally, learn more about what it means to create a corporation: becoming an Inc., a Corps. or an LLC. It's pretty easy to do, and it can make it a lot easier to get funding. Put some thought into the name you choose. Some businesses are much more likely to get loans. With a good business plan, a few bank statements, and all of your corporation documents in order, you can qualify for a loan to buy one of the businesses we just talked about.

DIVERSIFY YOUR INCOME

I've heard it said that your average millionaire has seven sources of income. I don't know if that's true, and even if it is, I don't know that I agree 100% with that approach. For me, seven sources of income would mean seven different things that I have to give my undivided attention to. And that's too much for one person to commit to without something failing.

"Baby" businesses, as I like to call new ventures, are like actual babies and demand the most attention. Imagine having seven newborns. Not impossible, but not ideal. If you have a choice, pouring everything you have into one "baby" at a time is what will give you the greatest chance of success.

But I do agree with the goal of having multiple sources of income. In other words, diversifying where your money comes from, one baby at a time.

My first business was my personal injury law firm. Technically, I do some side work in the legal industry as another source of income, but I don't consider it diversifying if you stay in the same field. Plus I don't have a seprate company or corporation.

So, real estate became my second source of income. It made sense because I grew up learning about construction from my father. Fixing and flipping homes was how I first dabbled in this industry.

Now though, I've also become a corporate real estate broker, helping others with short sales before their home goes into fore-closure, or listing the sale, purchase or rental of properties, both residential and commercial. And I love it!

Sometimes your second source of income can be as much a part of your passion as the first. You love all your babies equally.

Then I also have an Independent Medical Exam business. This is diversifying in a way that benefits my law firm, one baby helping another. It gives me an edge because it allows me to actually help my competition while providing me with stability.

And allow me to introduce you to my newest baby, this book!

Having different businesses helps me to mitigate risk and create stability. So if I happen to have a bad year in real estate, I can count on my law firm income to see my family through.

Consider diversifying what you do so that your risks aren't quite as risky, and you always have a backup plan or safety net.

SALES

When it comes to being successful in business, no matter what business you're in, you need to understand the basics of sales. And get good at it!

For many people, when they hear the words "sales job," they run the other way. Because in lots of cases, you don't get much of a paycheck unless you make a sale. In other words, no stability. This can be scary, but it can also have its advantages.

Unlike most jobs, landing a sales gig is a great way to make something extra - a commission, a bonus - and to do it fast, without being tied to the same paycheck week after week. That's money you might be able to turn right around and invest.

Having some basic sales skills is pretty vital for a Ladyshark. Every business needs you to be a good seller, even if what you're selling is yourself – who you are and what you can do for your customers.

I had a client walk in one day looking for a new law firm to move his case to. He was leaving a really glamorous firm, like the one on the show *Suits*. And I couldn't figure out why he'd come into our little office looking for a change.

Then he explained that the other firm rarely answered his calls and didn't talk him through the problems when they did answer his calls. He wanted a law firm who could do for him what they said they would.

It didn't take me long for me to sell him on the fact that my firm could do that for him. We are in it for the people, and we are humble enough to baby and educate our clients from beginning to end.

INNOVATIVE INVESTING

Not having resources upfront doesn't have to limit your opportunities. For Ladysharks, it's all about creative problem-solving—finding alternative ways to invest. Even CDs at the bank can make you money by making your money work for you. Gain interest until you come up with a master plan.

So even if you only invest $500, in a few months that could grow to $600 or $700. And you just earned money instead of having your savings sit in a regular bank account at almost zero interest.

You might decide you want to look at investment properties as an extra source of income. But maybe you don't have the money for a down payment lying around, so you can't just buy something. Do you know someone who does? Consider every angle.

Ever heard of an assignment contract? Here's how those work.

Let's say someone agrees to buy a house, but before they officially own it, they decide to sell their agreement to buy the house to someone else for a higher price. The new buyer takes over the agreement and buys the house instead. It's like passing along the promise to buy the house to someone else who wants it more – and is willing to pay more for it. If you're the person who negotiates the deal, then you get a cut of the higher price. And without a real estate license or a degree!

Or maybe you can leverage your network of family and friends to pull together a group who can afford to invest. They give you a chunk of money with your promise to do all the hard work. Or what about finding a silent partner who has money to invest? Boom. Profit for whatever you have planned next. Just be careful of the fine print, and be sure to protect yourself with a solid contract.

When it comes to innovative investing, where there's a will, there's a way. Think outside of the box.

WHAT DOES IT EVEN MEAN TO BE RICH?

What does being rich mean? When you hear the word "millionaire," you might assume it means that person is rich. But depending on your expenses, a million dollars is not necessarily that much money these days.

How do I define being rich? Financial freedom and stability. Being able to live the life I want to live without being in perpetual fear that it's all going to go away. To be able to take care of my family. To have more assets than liabilities, and to keep the growth running like a machine. To make sure I'm able to go on vacation every once in a while, without putting myself in debt because of it.

So, technically, yes, based on that definition… I'm now rich.

But it's interesting because it's not like now that I have the financial freedom I worked so hard for, I sit around twiddling my thumbs all day. Or live at a tropical resort. Nope. I still work really hard – almost as hard as when I started. (Though I prioritize getting home earlier now, so that I can spend time with my family whenever possible.)

I work hard for the money that gives me the financial freedom I'm now enjoying, while I continue to work my ass off. Financial freedom is an ongoing journey, not a one-time trip.

You might be thinking: "Chrissy, do you like working so hard? Why don't you just relax?"

But you know what? I do like it. I think most Ladysharks enjoy the hustle. It's part of who we are. It's a fire inside where nothing is ever enough. So while I appreciate all that I have, the fire still burns.

IT'S UP TO YOU

One day you will reach exciting numbers: your first $10,000. Your first $100,000. But making your first million is a really big deal. And the way to get there is rarely by having a paycheck-to-paycheck job with no real option for making a little extra money on the side. No bonuses or commissions. No way to get ahead. So I try to give my employees opportunities to earn extra money whenever I can, as long as they are willing to hustle. Hard work does pay off!

Yes, you have to keep hustling. Complacency equals death for a Ladyshark. Maybe that sounds dramatic. Maybe that doesn't appeal to everyone. But if you're complacent, you're never going to grow.

Only you have the power to change your circumstances. Nothing is going to happen by itself, and no one is going to throw financial freedom into your lap.

A lot of people spend time complaining about their status, their position, their problems in life. But they don't do anything to change it. Obviously, I didn't write this book for those people. Complaining about things won't get you very far in life. It's not problem solving. You can complain, but then you have to think: What are you doing to make a change, to make things better? If you're living paycheck to paycheck, and it sucks… You have to do something besides complain, or nothing will ever change.

Don't let the question, "How do I get started?" hold you back. Start dreaming, start building. Budget, track, learn, and most importantly, don't let the fear of mistakes hold you back. Hone in on what you want, focus, and never lose track of your trajectory.

Your path to financial freedom is going to be full of ups and downs. But it's your life. Don't waste it. Your legacy depends on it. Embrace the lessons, celebrate the victories, and build that treasure chest!

LADYSHARKS YOU SHOULD KNOW

There are Ladysharks in every industry. And no matter what they do, they kick ass as they do it.

Here are a few who have inspired a lot of people over the years. You might know some of these Ladysharks, or you might want to get to know all of them!

Legal & Political Powerhouses

- **Judge Judy**: The badass Manhattan family court judge known for her no-nonsense attitude, sharp wit, and quick decision-making.
- **Ketanji Brown Jackson**: The brilliant, history-making first Black woman on the Supreme Court.
- **Malala Yousafzai**: The fearless Nobel Prize winner fighting for every girl's right to an education.
- **Greta Thunberg**: The young, bold climate warrior taking the world by storm.
- **Ruth Bader Ginsburg** (RIP): The legendary Supreme Court justice who was a total boss in the fight for gender equality and women's rights.
- **Amal Clooney**: The fierce human rights lawyer who's making waves in international law.

Literary Legends

- **J.K. Rowling**: The wizard behind Harry Potter, casting spells with her stories and charity work.
- **Margaret Atwood**: The literary genius famous for *The Handmaid's Tale* and more.
- **Amanda Gorman**: The youngest inaugural poet in U.S. history, a true wordsmith.
- **Gloria Steinem**: The journalist who's been a badass voice in feminist thought.

- **Maya Angelou**: Her words in *I Know Why the Caged Bird Sings* continue to inspire and empower.

Music Mavens
- **Rihanna**: Not just a music icon but a business mogul too.
- **Taylor Swift**: The singer-songwriter who turns her life into chart-topping hits and owns her own music.
- **Beyoncé**: The unstoppable force in music and culture.
- **Lizzo**: The queen of body positivity and self-love anthems.
- **J-Lo**: The multi-talented powerhouse who went from humble beginnings to conquer the worlds of music, film, television, and business.

Biz & Tech Trailblazers
- **Suze Orman**: The money guru who tells it like it is.
- **Melinda Gates**: Changing the world, one global health and education initiative at a time.
- **Katrina Lake**: The brain behind Stitch Fix, blending fashion with tech.
- **Sheryl Sandberg**: The Facebook COO who's all about women leading the way.
- **Susan Wojcicki**: The boss lady running YouTube.
- **Lori Greiner**: Shark Tank's "Queen of QVC" known for her eye for consumer products.

Sporty Superheroes
- **Serena Williams**: The tennis legend who's as fierce in advocating for women as she is on the court.
- **Megan Rapinoe**: The soccer star who's kicking goals for LGBTQ+ rights and equal pay.
- **Simone Biles**: The gymnastics genius flipping her way into history.

- **Danica Patrick**: Speeding past barriers in the male-dominated world of racing.
- **Billie Jean King**: The tennis icon who's been serving up gender equality for decades.

Health & Wellness Warriors
- **Brene Brown**: The guru of vulnerability and shame, teaching us to be our bravest selves.
- **Jillian Michaels**: The fitness powerhouse who's all about a balanced approach to health.
- **Glenn Doyle**: The author whose memoirs scream authenticity and self-liberation.
- **Jennifer Doudna**: The Nobel Prize-winning biochemist revolutionizing genetics with CRISPR.

SHARKS AND LADYSHARKS: MORE SIMILAR THAN YOU THINK

Have you ever hummed the Jaws theme when you're at the beach, just to watch people squirm? Just like sharks, sometimes Ladysharks get a bad rap.

The truth is, most people picture sharks as dangerous, scary beasts. And sometimes Ladysharks are seen that way too.

But you know what? I think sharks and Ladysharks have some pretty great positive traits in common:

Always Adapting
- Sharks have been kicking around for millions of years – they know how to survive.
- Ladysharks are the same – constantly shifting gears to work with all sorts of people and all kinds of challenges.

Super Efficient
- Sharks waste zero energy when hunting.
- Ladysharks have to be the same – smart about their time and resources in order to pull off big wins.

Tenacious AF
- Sharks have to keep moving in order to breathe. They just keep going.
- Ladysharks, too. They're all about digging deep and refusing to give up.

Bouncing Back
- Sharks shed teeth like it's no big deal.
- Ladysharks take some hits too, maybe even more since they're always pushing boundaries. The secret is getting back up fast.

Super Focused

- Sharks lock onto their target and that's it.
- Ladysharks do that with their goals – nothing else matters until they get there.

A Balancing Act

- Sharks actually help keep the ocean healthy.
- Every Ladyshark does the same in her own world – shooting for a balance between work and life.

While I may not be heading off to go swimming with actual sharks any time soon, as a Ladyshark, I'm psyched to have so much in common with a strong, respected animal. So psyched that I made it part of my brand.

THE LADYSHARK WORKBOOK

Hey, you just made it through my whole book. All eight steps!

Or maybe you didn't. Maybe you just skipped to the end because, in true Ladyshark fashion, you wanted to get straight to the point, see the how-to part, and get started.

Either way, I'd like to say, WOW! Job well done! And thank you!

So now what?

I like direction when I'm on a mission, so I created a workbook with questions to ask yourself to kickstart your own Ladyshark journey!

Set aside some quiet, uninterrupted time to focus and answer each question. Return to these questions again and again as you Ladyshark your way through life, building the life you want.

QUESTION 1:

How can I understand my finances better?

Experiment: Take a close look at where your money goes. Make your necessities list. Figure out your recurring bills. Print everything out on paper if you have to. See if there are ways you can cut back, even just temporarily. A streaming service? That 3rd drink? Every little bit can help.

Then pay attention to how it feels for you in the next week or two. What did you miss? And what did you not miss at all? Maybe you found some new, cheaper favorites? Or maybe you realized you had some completely unnecessary expenses. The faster you save capital for the next chapter, the closer you'll be to financial freedom.

Understand Your Finances:
Step 1: Here are a few things you should start asking yourself immediately:
- How much do I make?
- How much do I spend?
- What's in my checking account?
- Am I saving money?
- What does being rich mean to me?

Step 2: Make a financial plan. Design the kind of life you're hoping to lead - what having financial freedom would look like for you.

- Does it mean being able to have someone clean your house? Great, add that to your list.
- Does it mean driving a certain kind of car? Great. Put that down.

Everyone's list is going to look different. But making that list is the only way to know what you're working so hard for.

Step 3: Check your credit, like, now…and protect your credit score because it's sacred. Even with cash, it can be useless if you don't have good credit. Go to Credit Karma, Experian, TransUnion, or LifeLock to learn more.

If your credit is bad, commit to fixing it immediately. You HAVE to have good credit if you want to be able to invest and make money. So get those finances organized!

And never let money sit in your savings account doing nothing – especially if you owe money on credit cards where you're losing money.

QUESTION 2:

How am I learning?

Do This: Start a "Cool Stuff I Learned" notebook (or a digital note on your phone). Every day, write down anything new you learned, no matter how big or small.

After a month, flip through and see what inspires you. Did you spend more time learning fun facts or studying new life skills? Would you like to do more of either or both? What classes could you take to gain skills to convert to money?

QUESTION 3:

Where could I work harder?

Try This: Think about an area of your life where you've been slacking off or wish you had done better. Give it focused extra attention for a week. Keep a super simple diary along the way as you give it more effort.

Was it as hard as you thought it would be? Did anything get easier? How much closer did you get to your goals after just one week?

QUESTION 4:

Where can I follow up?

Activity: Make a To Do List of how you might follow up on ideas or with specific people. Then pick the top three that make you feel excited or nervous or uncomfortable. Sketch out a plan of what it would take for you to tackle each of them. Then give it your best go.

Try to do all three. Then reward yourself by jotting down what it felt like to check them off your list. How did that help you get closer to your goal?

QUESTION 5:

What's a problem I can try to solve?

Challenge: Pinpoint an issue you're dealing with at home or at work or anywhere in your life that you must overcome to achieve success. Name it. Write it down. Then dream up a plan to fix it, baby step by baby step. Check off each step as you go until you have a list full of checkmarks. Each one matters. Each one is moving you forward.

QUESTION 6:

Who can I connect with?

Mission: Find yourself a mentor and connect with them. Some-one who inspires you to want to work harder and to be the Lady-shark you know you are. Make a list of people who you'd like to be able to call a mentor. And then let them know! They can't support you if they don't know you'd like them to.

Tell them why you're inspired by them, and thank them for blazing a trail for you. It's not important whether or not you hear back from them, or whether or not they are able to become true mentors to you. What's important is that you keep being creative about connecting with the kinds of people you want to be.

QUESTION 7:

Where could I use a backup plan?

Task: Think of something important you're currently working on. Now imagine what might possibly happen to mess it up. Come up with a "just in case" plan, or even two. Maybe it's a side hustle? A new business venture?

Note how it feels to have those new options in your corner just in case. Add to your master notebook – not just your plan A, but plan B, C and D. Hopefully you won't need them, but you've got them to turn to if you do. There are lots of paths on the road to financial freedom.

QUESTION 8:

What can I ask for?

Goal: Teamwork makes the dream work. Is there something you could use some help with? An issue at work? Moving a couch? A tricky conversation with a friend? Think about who might help you out and make the time to ask them. Keep it light. Keep it simple. You might be surprised how often people are willing to lend a hand.

QUESTION 9:

What are my 3 top priorities?

Reflection: Pretend you're explaining to a child the three things that matter most to you right now. Tell them the story about why each of them is so important to you. Tell them how you keep them in focus in your life.

QUESTION 10:

What is the story I want the world to know me for?

Project: Imagine your life as a book or movie. What's the main plot? What's the genre? Write a one to two sentence summary of it. Sketch or use AI to make a poster for it. Find some songs for the soundtrack of your life. Cast a few actors in the important roles. Remember: You're molding your own legacy.

Thanks again, Ladysharks! I wish you all the best!!
And you know what?
If you have questions, or if I can help you out,
get in touch at
www.theladyshark.com

Acknowledgments

I'm so grateful to Jen Tate, who tapped into her own Ladyshark-ness to craft this book with me. I couldn't have done it without her!

I would also like to extend my deepest thanks to:
- My devoted editor, MeiMei Fox, and the team at Your Best-selling Book.
- Megan and Ira at TSPA - The Self Publishing Agency.
- And, the PR experts at Nardi Media.

Their contributions have been invaluable in bringing this project to life.

A special thanks to:
- Samuel Paredes who put in years of hard work bringing my shark vision to fruition.
- Michael Caseau who led me to my team so I could finally spread my Ladyshark words of wisdom.
- And to everyone who has supported me on my Ladyshark journey.

About the Author

Chrissy Grigoropoulos is the founding partner of The Grigoropoulos Law Group (GLG) and the CEO of IME Sharks. She also has been the principal realtor of Property Shark Realty since 2015.

As a self-made millionaire, Grigoropoulos has appeared as a personal finance expert and real estate thought leader on live national TV from the floor of the NY Stock Exchange, as well as on Fox News and Yahoo! Finance. She has been a guest on numerous top-ranked podcasts, including She's Brave, Suburban Warrior and Path to Mastery.

Grigoropoulos founded her own law firm, GLG, while still in her 20s. She handles large exposure personal injury lawsuits, high-profile criminal defense, and workers' compensation cases coupled with third-party actions. As a litigator and trial attorney, she has vast experience in criminal defense. She also appears as trial counsel for other law firms, litigating their personal injury lawsuits in New York courts, and at arbitrations and mediations.

From an early age, Grigoropoulos worked hard to achieve her goals. Notably, she finished high school at the age of 16 and received her BA from St. Joseph's College at 19. She earned her JD from Western Michigan University's Thomas M. Cooley Law School in 2013.